Facilitating with Ease!

A Step-by-Step

Guidebook with

Customizable

Worksheets

on CD-ROM

Ingrid Bens, M.Ed.

Copyright © 2000 by Jossey-Bass Inc., Publishers, 350 Sansome Street, San Francisco, California 94104.

ISBN: 0-7879-5194-3

Library of Congress Cataloging-in-Publication Data

Bens, Ingrid,
    Facilitating with ease! : a step-by-step guidebook with customizable worksheets on CD-Rom / Ingrid Bens.
        p.   cm.
    Originally published: Sarasota, Fla. : Participative Dynamics, 1997.
    Includes bibliographical references.
    ISBN 0-7879-5194-3
    1. Teams in the workplace. 2. Group facilitation. I. Title
HD66.B445 2000
658.4'036 21—dc21   99-045515

Printed in the United States of America

Jossey-Bass books and products are available through most bookstores. To contact Jossey-Bass directly, call (888) 378-2537, fax to (800) 605-2665, or visit our website at www.josseybass.com.

Substantial discounts on bulk quantities of Jossey-Bass books are available to corporations, professional associations, and other organizations. For details and discount information, contact the special sales department at Jossey-Bass.

Printing 10 9 8 7 6 5 4 3 2

This book is printed on acid-free, recycled stock that meets or exceeds the minimum GPO and EPA requirements for recycled paper.

Table of Contents

Chapter 4 – Creating Participation

Chapter 5 – Facilitating Conflict

Chapter 6 – Effective Decision Making

Chapter 7 – Meeting Management

Chapter 8 – Process Tools for Facilitators

Chapter 9 – Process Designs

Introduction

It's impossible to be part of an organization today and not attend meetings. Staff meetings, project meetings, task force meetings, planning and coordinating meetings. . . the list is endless. The worst thing about many of these meetings is that they're poorly run and waste people's valuable time.

Over the past decade, there's been a growing recognition that effective meetings happen when proper attention has been paid to the *process* elements and when the proceedings are skillfully facilitated.

For a long time, *facilitation* has been a rather vague and poorly understood practice, mastered only by human resources HR types. This situation needs to change. We're now spending so much time in meetings and being asked to achieve so many important goals in teams that there's a growing need for skilled facilitation throughout our organizations and our communities.

Instead of being relegated to HR, facilitation is fast becoming a core competency for anyone who's on a team, leading a task force, heading up a committee, or managing a department. All of these people need to be able to create dynamic group settings in which people truly collaborate and make sound decisions.

Facilitation is also a central skill for today's managers, who are riding wave after wave of change. New demands are being placed on them. At the same time, the old command and control model of supervision, which worked for decades, isn't working anymore.

To get the most from people today, leaders have to know how to create buy-in, generate active participation and empower people to take charge.

To keep pace, tomorrow's leaders need to be coaches, mentors, sponsors and teachers. At the core of each of these new roles is the skill of facilitation.

> *With its focus on asking instead of telling, listening and building consensus, facilitation is the embodiment of the new leadership ideal and a core skill for all leaders!*

The Goal of this Book

This practical workbook has been created to make core facilitation tools and techniques readily available to the growing number of people who want to improve their process skills. It represents materials and ideas that have been collected, tested and refined during over twenty years of active facilitation in all types of settings.

While it builds on the theories of organization development pioneers such as Chris Argyris, Donald Schon, and Edgar Schein, this workbook doesn't aim to be theoretical. Instead, its focus is on providing the reader with the most commonly used process tools, in a simple and accessible format. This is not so much a book to be read, as one to be used!

The Audience

This workbook contains valuable information for anyone facilitating group interactions. This is a huge constituency. It includes:

- team leaders and team members
- project and task force leaders
- any supervisor or manager who holds staff meetings
- community development practitioners
- community leaders working on neighborhood projects
- teachers in traditional classroom settings
- adult educators creating learning organizations
- mediators engaged in "interest-based bargaining"
- marketing consultants who run focus groups
- quality consultants leading process improvement initiatives
- therapists who convene support groups
- consultants making interventions or managing conflicts

- anyone teaching others to facilitate
- anyone called on to lead a discussion or run a meeting.

For the sake of clarity, many of the strategies and techniques in this book are described from the perspective of an external facilitator. These same tools work equally well, however, whether the facilitator comes from inside or outside of the group. The book also mentions team leaders and workplace teams often, but again, the tools and applications apply to all and any facilitation situation.

Content Overview

The book is organized into nine chapters. Checklists and tools have not be collected in an appendix, but are located throughout each chapter, near the related materials.

Chapter 1 outlines what facilitation is and its main applications. It differentiates process from content, and outlines the core practices. It also addresses facilitation issues such as neutrality, how assertive a facilitator can be and how to balance the role of the group leader with that of the facilitator.

Chapter 1 also describes who can best facilitate in various situations. It provides information about the language of facilitation, the principles of giving and receiving feedback, plus a thumbnail sketch of the best and worst practices of facilitators. At the end of the chapter, there are several observation sheets and a four-level skills self-assessment, useful to anyone hoping for feedback on current skills.

Chapter 2 explores the stages of a planned facilitation. It describes the importance of each step in the facilitation process: assessment, design, feedback, refinement and final preparation. Helpful checklists are also provided to guide the start, middle and end of any facilitation session.

Chapter 3 focuses on knowing your participants and provides information about the four most commonly used needs-assessment techniques. Sample assessment questions and surveys are provided. This chapter also discusses the differences between facilitating groups and facilitating teams and passes along strategies for getting any group to behave more like an effective team. The creation of team norms is discussed, along with an overview of the team growth stages and the corresponding facilitation strategies that work best at each stage.

Chapter 4 begins with a frank discussion of the many reasons people are often less than enthusiastic to be involved in a meeting or workshop and provides tested strategies for overcoming these blocks, including ideas on gaining buy-in. High participation techniques are also shared, along with a training plan to encourage effective meeting behaviors in members.

Chapter 5 deals with facilitative strategies for handling both conflict and resistance. It begins with an overview of the difference between healthy debates and dysfunctional arguments. It goes on to share techniques that encourage healthy debates and the steps in the conflict-management model. Special attention is paid to facilitator strategies for venting emotions. The five conflict-management options are then explored and placed into the context of which are most appropriate for facilitators.

Chapter 5 also provides a three-part format for wording interventions that help group members assess their situation and make improvements. Also described are the two approaches a facilitator can choose when confronted with resistance and illustrates why one is superior. At the end of the chapter, nine common facilitator dilemmas and their solutions are presented, along with the rationale for assuming a confrontational stance in those situations in which the group is plagued by hidden agendas, lack of trust or conventional thinking.

Chapter 6 delves into the complexities of decision making. It begins with an overview of the symptoms, causes and cures for poor decisions. A survey is provided with which a group can assess its current decision-making effectiveness. Six different methods for reaching decisions are described and differentiated. The pros, cons, and uses of each approach are explored, along with an expanded discussion of consensus building. At the end of the chapter there's a discussion of the behaviors that help decision effectiveness and an overview of the steps in the systematic consensus-building process.

Chapter 7 focuses on meeting management. There's a useful checklist and meeting effectiveness diagnostic that lets groups assess whether or not their meetings are working. There's also a chart that outlines the symptoms and cures for common meeting ills. The fundamentals of meeting management are outlined, with special emphasis on the role of the facilitator as compared to the traditional chairperson role. Both mid-point checks and exit surveys are explained, and samples are provided.

Chapter 8 contains the essential process tools that are fundamental to all facilitation activities. These include: visioning, brainstorming, gap analysis, decision grids, priority setting, systematic problem solving, survey feedback, sequential questioning, force-field analysis, multi-voting,

trouble shooting, needs and offers negotiation and root cause analysis. Each tool is described along with step-by-step directions for its use in groups.

Chapter 9 pulls it all together by providing ten sample process designs, complete with facilitator notes. These facilitator notes describe each meeting design in detail and set an example for how facilitators should prepare their design notes. The ten samples are the most commonly requested facilitations and provide the reader with graphic illustrations of the level of detail a facilitator needs to consider before stepping in front of any group.

After twenty years of experience as a consultant, project manager, team leader and trainer, I'm totally convinced that it's impossible to build teams, consistently achieve consensus or run effective decision-making meetings, without highly developed facilitation skills. The good news is that these skills can be mastered by anyone! I hope you find *Facilitating with Ease!* to be a valuable resource in gaining this important skill.

Sarasota, Florida **Ingrid Bens, M.Ed.**
May 1999

Questions Answered in this Book

What is facilitating? When do I use it?

What is the role of the facilitator?

What are the main tools and techniques?

What are the values and attitudes of a facilitator?

How neutral do I really need to be?

How assertive am I allowed to be?

How do I size up my participants?

How do I get everyone to participate?

How do I overcome people's reluctance to open up?

What's the difference between a group and a team?

How can I get a group to act like a team?

What do I do if a group is very cynical?

What do I do if I encounter high resistance?

What if there's zero buy-in?

What are my options for dealing with conflict?

What if the meeting falls apart and I lose control?

What decision-making techniques are available?

Why is consensus the best method to use?

What can go wrong in making decisions?

Should I defend myself if attacked?

How do I make sure that discussions achieve closure?

How do I balance the roles of chairperson and facilitator?

What facilitation tools are available?

How do I know whether the meeting is going well?

How can I design a well-balanced meeting?

Some Definitions

Facilitator:

One who contributes *structure* and *process* to interactions so groups are able to function effectively and make high-quality decisions. A helper and enabler whose goal is to support others as they achieve exceptional performance.

Content:

The topics or subjects under discussion at any meeting. Also referred to as the task, the decisions made, or the issues explored.

Process:

The structure, framework, methods and tools used in interactions. Refers to the climate or spirit established, as well as the style of the facilitator.

Intervention:

An action or set of actions that aims to improve the functioning of a group.

Plenary:

A large group session held to share the ideas developed in separate subgroups.

Norms:

A set of rules created by group members with which they mutually agree to govern themselves.

Group:

A collection of individuals who come together to share information, coordinate their efforts, or achieve a task, but who mainly pursue their own individual goals and work independently.

Team:

A group of individuals who are committed to achieving a common goal, who support each other, who fully utilize member resources, and who have closely linked roles.

Chapter 1
Understanding Facilitation

*I*n many organizations, the idea of using a neutral third party to manage and improve meetings is now taking root. The result: the emergence of a new and important role in which the person who manages the meeting no longer participates in the discussion or tries to influence the outcome. Instead, he or she stays out of the discussion in order to focus on how the meeting is being run. Instead of offering opinions, this person provides participants with structure and tools. Instead of promoting a point of view, he or she manages participation to ensure that everyone is being heard. Instead of making decisions and giving orders, he or she supports the participants in identifying *their own* goals and developing *their own* action plans.

More and more organizations are now adopting this role within their meetings. In all of the above examples the meeting manager was acting as a *facilitator*.

What Is Facilitation?

Facilitation is a way of providing leadership without taking the reins. As a facilitator, your job is to get others to assume responsibility and to take the lead.

Here's an example: Your employees bring you a problem, but instead of offering them solutions, you offer them a method with which *they* can develop their own answers. You attend the meetings to guide the members through their discussions, step-by-step, encouraging them to reach their own conclusions.

Rather than being a player, a facilitator acts more like a referee. That means you watch the action, more than participate in it. You control which activities happen. You keep your finger on the pulse and know when to move on or wrap things up. Most important, you help members define and reach their goals.

A meeting without a facilitator is about as effective as a team trying to have a game without a referee.

What Does a Facilitator Do?

Facilitators make their contribution by:
- helping the group define its overall goal, as well as its specific objectives
- helping members assess their needs and create plans to meet them
- providing processes that help members use their time efficiently to make high-quality decisions
- guiding group discussion to keep it on track
- making accurate notes that reflect the ideas of members
- helping the group understand its own processes in order to work more effectively

- making sure that assumptions are surfaced and tested
- supporting members in assessing their current skills, as well as building new skills
- using consensus to help a group make decisions that take all members' opinions into account
- supporting members in managing their own interpersonal dynamics
- providing feedback to the group, so that they can assess their progress and make adjustments
- managing conflict using a collaborative approach
- helping the group communicate effectively
- helping the group access resources from inside and outside the group
- creating an environment in which members enjoy a positive, growing experience, while they work to attain group goals
- fostering leadership in others by sharing the responsibility for leading the group
- teaching and empowering others to facilitate

What Does a Facilitator Believe?

All facilitators believe that two heads are better than one and, that to do a good job, people need to be taken seriously and play a part in whatever they're doing.

To be a facilitator, *you must firmly believe* that:
- people are intelligent, capable and want to do the right thing
- groups can make better decisions than any one person can make alone
- everyone's opinion is of equal value, regardless of rank or position
- people are more committed to the ideas and plans that they have helped to create
- participants can and will act responsibly in assuming true accountability for their decisions
- groups can manage their own conflicts, behaviors and relationships if they are given the right tools and training
- the *process*, if well designed and honestly applied, can be trusted to achieve results

In contrast to the old notion of leadership, in which the leader was viewed as the most important person at the table, a facilitator puts the members first. Members decide what the goals are, make the decisions, implement the action plans, and hold themselves accountable for achieving results. The facilitator's contribution is to offer the right methods and tools at the right time.

Facilitating is ultimately about shifting responsibility from the leader to the members, from management to employees. By playing a *process* role, you encourage the members to take charge of the *content*.

What Sorts of Assignments Do Facilitators Handle?

As a facilitator you could be asked to design and lead a wide variety of meetings. These might include*:

- a strategic planning session
- a session to clarify objectives and create detailed results indicators
- a priority-setting meeting
- a team-building session
- a program review/evaluation session
- a meeting to negotiate team roles and responsibilities
- a problem-solving meeting

- a meeting to share feedback and improve performance
- a communications/liaison meeting
- a focus group to gather input on a new program or product

Differentiating Between Process and Content

The two words you'll hear over and over again in facilitation are *process* (how) and *content* (what). They are the two dimensions of any interaction between people.

The *content* of any meeting is *what* is being discussed: the task at hand, the subjects being dealt with, and the problems being solved. The *content* is expressed in the agenda and the words that are spoken. Because it's the verbal portion of the meeting, the content is obvious and typically consumes the attention of the members.

Process deals with *how* things are being discussed: the methods, procedures, format and tools used. The *process* also includes the style of the interaction, the group dynamics and the climate that is established. Because the *process* is often silent, it is harder to pinpoint. It is the aspect of most meetings that is largely unseen and often ignored, while people are focused on the *content*.

A facilitator's job is to manage the process and leave the "content" to the participants.

Content	Process
What	**How**
The subjects for discussion	The methods & procedures
The task	How relations are maintained
The problems being solved	The tools being used
The decisions made	The rules or norms set
The agenda items	The group dynamics
The goals	The climate

Sample agendas for a wide range of meetings have been provided in Chapter 9.

When a meeting leader offers an opinion with the intent of influencing the outcome of discussions, she or he is acting as the "content leader."

In contrast, a facilitator's job is to manage the *process* and leave *content* to the participants. When a meeting leader is neutral on the content and actively orchestrates the action, he or she is acting as the "process leader" or facilitator.

At first glance, facilitation may seem like a rather vague set of "warm and fuzzy," people-oriented beliefs. But as you'll learn, it's actually a very well-defined set of practices with a rich set of tools and techniques. Once you understand these techniques and learn how to apply them, you'll immediately see substantial improvement in the overall performance of any group.

Facilitation Tools

As a facilitator you'll have an extensive set of tools at your disposal. These tools fall into two categories: *Core Practices* and *Process Tools*.

The Core Practices, which are rooted in the manner, style and behavior of the facilitator, include:

- staying neutral
- listening actively
- asking questions
- paraphrasing

- synthesizing ideas
- staying on track
- giving and receiving feedback

- testing assumptions
- collecting ideas
- providing summaries

The effectiveness of any of these practices depends on how you handle yourself.

The *Process Tools,* which are structured activities that provide a clear sequence of steps, include:

- Visioning
- Brainstorming
- Anonymous Brainstorming

- Force-Field Analysis
- Gap Analysis
- Multi-Voting
- Priority Setting

- Root-Cause Analysis
- Decision Grids
- Systematic Problem Solving

Understanding each of these tools and how to use them is a vital part of any facilitator's job. In Chapter 8, you'll find detailed step-by-step instructions on how to apply these most frequently used process tools.

Core Practices Overview

Regardless of which type of process you're facilitating, all facilitators need to be constantly using the core practices:

Stay neutral on content – your job is to focus on the *process* role and avoid the temptation of offering opinions about the topic under discussion. You should use questions and suggestions to offer ideas that spring to mind, but never impose opinions on the group.

Listen actively – look people in the eye, use attentive body language and paraphrase what they are saying. Aways make eye contact with people while they

The best tool you've got as a facilitator is yourself.

speak, when paraphrasing what they have just said, and when summarizing their key ideas. Also use eye contact to let people know they can speak next, and to prompt the quiet ones in the crowd to participate.

Ask questions – this is the most important tool you possess. Questions test assumptions, invite participation, gather information, and probe for hidden points. Effective questioning allows you to delve past the symptoms to get at root causes.

Paraphrase to clarify – this involves repeating what people say to make sure they know they are being heard, to let others hear their points a second time, and to clarify key ideas. (i.e. *"Are you saying …? Am I understanding you to mean…?"*)

Synthesize ideas – don't just record individual ideas of participants. Instead, get people to comment and build on each other's thoughts to ensure that the ideas recorded on the flip chart represent collective thinking. This builds consensus and commitment. (i.e. *"Alice, what would you add to Jeff's comments?"*)

Stay on track – set time guidelines for each discussion. Appoint a time keeper inside the group to use a timer and call out milestones. Point out the digression if discussion has veered off topic. *"Park"* all off-topic comments and suggestions on a separate "Parking Lot" sheet posted on a nearby wall, to be dealt with later.

Give and receive feedback – periodically *"hold up a mirror"* to help the group *"see"* itself so it can make corrections. (i.e. *"Only two people are engaged in this discussion, while three others are reading. What's this telling us we need to do?"*) Also ask for and accept feedback about the facilitation. (i.e. *"Are we making progress? How's the pace? What can I do to be more effective?"*)

Test assumptions – you need to bring the assumptions people are operating under out into the open and clarify them, so that they are clearly understood by everyone. These assumptions may even need to be challenged before a group can explore new ground. (i.e. *"John, on what basis are you making the comment that 'Bob's idea is too narrow in focus'?"*)

Collect ideas – keep track of both emerging ideas and final decisions. Make clear and accurate summaries on a flipchart or electronic board so everyone can see the notes. Notes should be brief and concise. they must always reflect what the participants actually said, rather than your interpretation of what they said.

Summarize clearly – a great facilitator listens attentively to everything that is said, and then offers concise and timely summaries. Summarize when you want to revive a discussion that has ground to a halt, or to end a discussion when things seem to be wrapping up.

The Core Practices make up the foundation of the facilitator's style.

Label sidetracks – it's your responsibility to let the group members know when they're off track. They can then decide to pursue the sidetrack, or stop their current discussion and get back to the agenda. (i.e. *"We are now discussing something that isn't on our agenda. What does the group want to do?"*)

Park it – at every meeting, tape a flip chart sheet to a wall to record all side-track items. Later, these items can be reviewed for inclusion in a future agenda. "Parking lot" sheets let you capture ideas that may be important later, while staying on track.

Use the spell-check button – most people are nervous enough about writing on flip charts without having to worry that they're spelling every word right. You'll relax everyone by drawing a *spell-check button* at the top right corner of every flip sheet. Tell participants they *can spell creatively, since pressing the spell-check button automatically eliminates all errors.*

Focus on Questioning

The importance of knowing how and when to ask great probing questions can't be stressed enough. In fact, effective questioning is *the key* facilitative technique. As a facilitator, you can never ask too many questions.

Questions invite participation. They get people thinking about issues from a different perspective. Even when acting as a neutral facilitator, you can share your good ideas by turning them into questions. Questions are also essential for getting feedback from participants about how things are going.

Effective questioning means:
- *Asking the right questions at the right time* — select the right type of question and phrase it so that it solicits the best possible response. Then, direct it to the right person.

IF YOU WANT TO ...	THEN ...
Stimulate everyone's thinking	Direct the question to the group
Allow people to respond voluntarily or avoid putting an individual on the spot	Ask a question such as *"What experiences have any of you had with this problem?"*
Stimulate one person to think and respond	Direct the question to that individual. *"How should we handle this, Bill?"*
Tap the known resources of an "expert" in the group	Direct the question to that person. *"Mary, you have had a lot of experience in applying these regulations with customers. What would you do in this case?"*

- *Handling answers to questions* – reinforce all correct answers positively. Be careful, however, when praising ideas, not to go overboard and compromise your neutrality by over-praising any one point of view. Be careful to acknowledge the efforts of any respondent, regardless of the answer given; minimize potential embarrassment for wrong or incomplete answers. Tactful responses to wrong answers can include:

    > *"I can see how you came up with that."*
    > *"That's an interesting point. Who else has an idea?"*
    > *"You are on the right track. What other ideas do you have?"*

- *Responding to questions* – if someone asks you about the content, or directly asks for your views, you have three options:

    1. Redirect the question to someone likely to have the right answer or refer it to the whole group.
    2. Defer any questions that are beyond the scope of anyone present and commit to getting back to the group with an answer later.
    3. Provide the answer yourself only as a last resort, or when you are the only person who can come up with the right answer.

Question Types

There are two basic question types:

1. OPEN ENDED
2. CLOSED ENDED

Each has its uses:

TYPE OF QUESTION	DESCRIPTION	EXAMPLE
CLOSED	Requires a one-word answer Closes off discussion Usually begins with "is," "can," "how many," or "does"	*"Does everyone understand the changes we've discussed?"*
OPEN ENDED	Requires more than a "yes" or "no" answer Stimulates thinking Usually begins with "what," "how," "when," or "why"	*"What ideas do you have for explaining the changes to our customer?"*

> *Avoid the temptation to respond to direct questions. Answering them takes you out of the facilitator's role.*

Questioning Formats

When selecting questions to ask, there is a broad range you can choose from. It's important to understand how each of these question formats achieves a slightly different outcome.

Different types of questions create specific responses.

Fact-finding questions are targeted at verifiable data such as who, what, when, where, and how much. Use them to gather information about the current situation.

    i.e. *"What kind of computer equipment are you now using?"*
         "How much training did staff receive at the start?"

Feeling-finding questions ask for subjective information that gets at the participants' opinions, feelings, values and beliefs. They help you understand views. Usually contain words like think or feel.

    i.e. *"How do you feel about the effectiveness of the new equipment?"*
         "Do you think the staff felt they received enough training?"

Tell-me-more questions can help you find out more about what the participants are saying. They encourage the speaker to provide more details.

    i.e. *"Tell me more?" "Can you elaborate on that?"*
         "Can you be more specific?"

Best/least questions help you understand potential opportunities in the present situation. They let you test for the outer limits of participants' wants and needs.

    i.e. *"What is the best thing about receiving a new computer?"*
         "What is the worst thing about the new equipment?"

Third-party questions help uncover thoughts in an indirect manner. They're designed to help people express sensitive information.

    i.e. *"Some people find that computer training is too time consuming. How does that sound to you?"*
         "There is some concern about overly autocratic managers in many factories. Can you relate to that concern?"

"Magic wand" questions let you explore people's true desires. Also known as "crystal ball" questions, these are useful in temporarily removing obstacles from a person's mind.

    i.e. *"If time and money were no obstacle, what sort of a computer system would you design for the department?"*

Sample Probing Questions

The following sample questions are designed to delve more deeply into a problem situation.

- How would you describe the current situation in this department?
- How would your most important customer describe it?
- How would a senior manager describe it?
- How long has this situation been going on?
- How do you feel about the situation?
- Why hasn't the problem been solved?
- Who wants change to take place? Who does not?
- Who contributes to the problem?
- How do you contribute to the problem?
- If the problem were totally resolved, what would the situation look like?

On a scale of 1 to 5, how serious would you say this problem is?

1	2	3	4	5
not serious at all		somewhat serious		very serious

- What are the most significant barriers to solving this problem?
- What are the parameters of this initiative? (time, money, materials)
- Are any solutions going to be taboo or unacceptable?
- How would you rate the overall level of commitment to making changes that have been agreed to?

1	2	3	4	5
Low		Medium		High

Questioning: Do's and Don'ts

DO	DON'T
Ask clear, concise questions covering a single issue	Ask rambling, ambiguous questions that cover multiple issues
Ask challenging questions that will stimulate thought	Ask questions that don't provide an opportunity for thought
Ask reasonable questions based on what people know	Ask questions that most people can't answer
Ask honest and relevant questions	Ask "trick" questions designed to fool them

It's a good idea to plan a set of questions before starting a facilitation.

Managing the Flip Chart

A flip chart may look innocent enough, but remember that these three-legged beasts can trip you, make your handwriting look like kindergarten scrawl, and make even familiar spelling impossible to recall. Here are some definite *do's* and *don'ts* about flip charts.

DO	DON'T
Write down exactly what members say. While their comments have to be edited somewhat, always use their key words. Check to make sure that what is written captures the meaning expressed.	Write down your personal interpretation of things. These are their notes. If unsure, ask "What should I write down?"
Use verbs and make phrases fairly complete. For example, writing "work group" is not as helpful as "work group to meet Monday at 10 a.m." Always be sure the flip chart can convey meaning, even to someone who was not at the meeting.	Worry about spelling. If you make a fuss, it will inhibit members from getting up and taking a turn at facilitating.
Talk and write at the same time. This is necessary in order to maintain a good pace. Practiced facilitators can write one thing and be asking the next question.	Hide behind the flip chart or talk to it. Unless you are writing, stand squarely beside it, facing the members when reading back notes.
Move around and act alive. There is nothing worse than a facilitator who acts as though he or she is chained to the flip chart. If an important point is being made, walk closer to the person who is talking so you can better pay attention.	Stand passively at the flip chart while a long discussion is going on without writing anything down. Ideas don't need to be in complete sentences before recording them. Make note of key words and ideas. Comprehensive statements can be formulated later.
Write in black, blue or some other dark color. Use fairly large letters so it can be read from the back of the room.	Use script unless you have great handwriting. Avoid red and other pale pastels that are impossible to see from any distance.
Post flip sheets around the room so that people can keep track of what has been discussed.	Monopolize the flip chart.
Whenever appropriate, let others take over both large and small group facilitation. This builds commitment and reinforces the idea that this isn't the facilitator's meeting.	Monopolize managing the meeting process.

The Language of Facilitation

A particular style of language has evolved as a part of facilitation. These techniques are especially important when it comes to commenting on people's behavior without sounding critical or judgmental. The main language techniques are:

- paraphrasing
- describing feelings
- reporting behavior
- perception checking

Paraphrasing involves describing, in your own words, what another person's remarks convey.

> *"If I understand you correctly, you are saying..."*
> *"Is this an accurate understanding of your point...?"*
> *"What you are saying is..."*

You should be paraphrasing continuously, especially if the discussion starts to spin in circles, or if people are getting heated. This repetition assures participants that their ideas are being heard. New facilitators often make the mistake of not paraphrasing enough.

Reporting behavior consists of stating the specific, observable actions of others without making accusations or generalizations about them as people or attributing motives to them.

> *"This is the third time you have rolled your eyes while I was presenting my ideas."*
> *"Two of you are reading and the others have grown very quiet."*

By describing specific behaviors, you give participants information about how their actions are being perceived. Feeding this information back to participants in a non-threatening manner opens the door for individuals to suggest actions to improve the existing situation.

Descriptions of feelings consist of specifying or identifying feelings by naming the feeling, using a metaphor, figure of speech, or action urge.

> *"I feel exhausted."* (naming)
> *"I feel like a kid on vacation."* (metaphor)
> *"I feel like a fly on the wall."* (figure of speech)
> *"I feel like jumping for joy!"* (action urge)

As a facilitator, you need to be in touch with how you're feeling and not be afraid to share those feelings with the group. It's very helpful to be honest with a group by telling them "I feel exhausted right now," or "I feel frustrated." This lets other people know that it's okay for them to express feelings.

Perception checking is describing what you perceive to be another person's inner state in order to check if you understand what he or she is feeling.

> *"You appear upset by the last comment that was made. Are you?"*
> *"You seem impatient. Are you anxious to move on to the next topic?"*

Perception checking is a very important tool. It lets you take the pulse of participants, who may be experiencing emotions that get in the way of their participation.

Mastering the language of facilitation will help you avoid sounding critical or judgmental when giving feedback.

Giving and Receiving Feedback

Every facilitator encounters situations that require feedback: perhaps the meeting is dragging or maybe people are exhausted and need a break; perhaps the group needs to improve its interpersonal behaviors. Managing feedback is an important facilitator responsibility. Feedback involves stopping the group's discussions to ask them to assess how it's going. Feedback can be about:

- how the meeting is going
- whether or not the goal is being achieved
- how members are conducting themselves
- how decisions are being made
- how the facilitator is doing

General Principles of Good Feedback

Feedback is always meant to be positive. Its goal is to improve the current situation or performance—its goal is never to criticize or offend. The structure of giving feedback is a reflection of this positive intent. No matter what form feedback takes, the following general principles always apply:

Be descriptive rather than evaluative – tell the other person what you notice or what has happened. Avoid all comments about him or her as a person.

Be specific instead of general – describe exactly what happened so that facts, not impressions, form the basis of the feedback.

Solicit feedback rather than impose it – ask the other person if you can give him or her feedback. If the person says no, respect that this may not be a good time. Collaborate to determine a more convenient time.

Time it – feedback should be given as soon as possible after the situation being described.

Focus on what can be changed – make suggestions for improvements that the person is capable of implementing.

Check the feedback – make sure your understanding is accurate and fair. Check with the person, or even with others, to avoid misjudging the situation.

Demonstrate caring – offer feedback with the positive intent of helping the other person.

Feedback Formats

Feedback can take a number of forms. You'll find sample formats throughout this book, but here are a few to get you started. You can:

- Hand out a survey for members to complete at a break. Then share results with the group for their analysis and action planning.
- Post selected questions on a flip chart. Ask members to rate each item. Discuss the results and look for solutions to any items that received low ratings.
- Ask group members to give each other written feedback in response to questions such as "What things are you doing well?" and/or, "What could you do to become even more effective?"

Feedback is essential to improving individual and group performance.

- Use *force-field analysis* (see Chapter 8, page 157) to discuss what is and is not going well with the whole group. The group then creates remedies for all of the things that aren't going well.
- Simply ask members to tell you how you're doing, and what you could do better.

The Eight-Step Feedback Process

Imagine you're at a meeting at which no one is putting the real issues on the table. Everyone is being polite and the problems of the group aren't being resolved. In this situation, the facilitator needs to stop the action and give feedback so the participants can resolve their problems and move on. It's never easy giving direct feedback, so use the right language and follow the steps outlined below:

Step 1: Ask permission to offer feedback

Asking permission lets people tell you if this is a bad time to hear feedback, and ensures that they're ready to pay careful attention. Asking permission is a way of signalling that you intend to give feedback.

> *"I'm going to stop this meeting now and give you some input that I think you need to hear. Is that OK?"*

Step 2: Describe specifically what you are observing

Give a clear and specific description of what you observed. Avoid generalizing, exaggerating or offering emotional accounts.

> *"During the interviews I held with more than half of you, the issue of some people not pulling their weight was mentioned by everyone as the most serious problem facing this team. We have been talking about team problems for two hours and yet no one has mentioned this issue."*

Step 3: Tell them about the direct impact of their actions

Describe the impact on individuals, the program or the department. Keep it very objective and don't get personal. Avoid blaming. Deal with the facts of the current situation.

> *"Since the issue of people not pulling their weight has not been mentioned, there's a good chance that these discussions are not going to resolve your most serious team problem."*

Step 4: Give the other person(s) an opportunity to explain

Listen actively, using attentive body language and paraphrasing key points.

> *"You're telling me that this problem isn't being discussed because it's too sensitive and people are concerned about offending each other."*

Sometimes feedback needs to be presented in a structured manner.

Step 5: Draw out ideas from the others

Frame the whole thing as a problem to be solved. Get people to offer their ideas. Remember that people are most likely to implement their own ideas. The more they self-prescribe, the better. Support their efforts at self-correction.

> *"What do you think we could do to make it feel safe enough so that this issue can be discussed? What guidelines will create the comfort we need?"*

Step 6: Offer specific suggestions for improvement

Make suggestions that will improve the situation. Wherever possible build on the ideas suggested by others.

> *"I think the guidelines you have come up with are excellent. I'd like to add a few ideas about how we can tackle this with sensitivity. Would this be OK?"*

Step 7: Summarize and express your support

Demoralizing people does not set the stage for improved performance; offering encouragement and ending on an optimistic note does.

> *"I want to thank you for being willing to tackle this tough subject."*

Step 8: Follow up

Make sure you end the feedback discussion with clear action steps. This ensures that the whole exercise doesn't need to be repeated later on.

> *"I'm going to stop the action in about an hour and check with you to see if we're now tackling our real problems and if the guidelines we set are working."*

The Language of Feedback

Here are a few more examples about language you can add to your tool kit to enhance the effectiveness of your feedback.

Openers to feedback:

> *"I'd like to give you input about …"*
> *"I have a concern about …"*
> *"I have information that I think you might be interested in."*
> *"I'd like to make a suggestion, if you're interested."*

Examples of feedback statements:

> *"Instead of (telling me what you think I should do), it would be better if you would (ask for my opinion)."*
> *"I know that you have a lot on your plate but I need (your full attention now)."*
> *"When you (keep on looking at your watch), I sense that you are/are not (getting any value out of this discussion)."*
> *"I'd like to propose that we try (openly discussing any problems) rather than trying to (keep them to ourselves)."*

Avoid "usually" or "always," as these words may offer more emphasis than you intended, or evoke a negative reaction. Never use assumptive labels that describe personal traits, such as "lazy," "thoughtless" and "sloppy." Instead, offer specific details about what the person did and when. Choose "how about," "let's try," or "would you consider?" in place of "should."

Tips for Receiving Feedback

If you've ever been involved in a feedback exercise, you know how difficult it can be – especially if you're on the receiving end. To make it easier for the giver, teach participants how to receive feedback in a non-defensive manner. Share the following tips:

Listen actively
Make eye contact with the speaker. Ask probing questions to make sure you understand what's being said.

Don't get emotional
Breathe deeply. Sit back. Adopt a relaxed body posture. Lower your voice. Speak slowly.

Don't get defensive
This isn't aimed at you personally. Understand the other person's perspective before presenting your side of the story. Ask for more details on points you don't agree with.

Accept the input
Even when you don't agree with all of it, there will be some good ideas – accept these. This shows respect for the other person's perspective.

Work to improve
Devote your energy to finding improvements rather than disputing observations. Do not put all of the burden for finding solutions on the other person. Offer ideas of your own.

How Neutral Do Facilitators Really Need to Be?

One of the toughest challenges as a facilitator is staying neutral when a group is making a decision you think is poor. You see them going down a dead end, but feel powerless to stop them – after all, you're supposed to be neutral!

While your objective is to focus on *process* and stay out of *content*, there are three techniques that you can use to give direction without compromising your neutral role.

1st Strategy – Ask Questions
If you have a good idea that might help the group, don't withhold it. Instead, offer the idea as a question. For example, you can ask *"What are the benefits of renting new computers as an interim strategy?"* The group can then consider this

As the facilitator you'll need to act as a model for receiving and accepting feedback.

option and accept or reject it. Your neutrality is maintained because you're not actually telling the group what to do. They still have the final say.

2nd Strategy – Offer Suggestions

Sometimes you'll have a good idea that the group hasn't considered, and even when you pose it as a question, it fails to make an impression. At this point, it's appropriate to ask the group to consider a suggestion from you. You might say: *"What about exploring the potential of renting computers for the next six months, until your new budget is approved?"* Although this might sound as if you've strayed into *content*, it's still facilitative as long as it sounds and feels like an offer, not an order. As long as the members retain the power to decide the issue, all you've done is help provide a new idea for their consideration.

3rd Strategy – Take Off the Facilitator's Hat

If the group is about to make a serious mistake, and all of the questioning and suggesting in the world hasn't worked to dissuade them, you may need to step out of your neutral role and tell the group what to do. In cases like these, it's important to first signal that you're stepping out of the facilitator role and clearly state that you are now offering advice. You might say: *"I need to step out of the role of facilitator for a minute and point out that renting computers is three times more cost effective than buying and doesn't stick you with outmoded hardware."* This role shift is legitimate only if you truly believe that the group is in grave danger of making a major mistake and you absolutely have to help them. Be careful though: leaping in and out of the facilitator's role too often causes confusion and distrust. Taking off the hat should be done very selectively and cautiously.

Neutrality in Different Situations

As a facilitator, you'll also have to reevaluate your neutrality depending on the situation. Remember, the bottom line lies in who has the power to decide. As long as your input doesn't influence members' ability to make decisions, you can stretch the limits of neutrality somewhat.

If, on the other hand, you overuse questions and suggestions to control outcomes, you will have overstepped the boundaries of the role to the detriment of the group. The following examples will give you an idea of how to tackle a variety of situations.

What if the group is making a serious mistake?

Groups often need to be allowed to make some of their own mistakes. However, if the mistake looks too serious to allow, you should first attempt to intervene in a facilitative capacity, rather than taking off your hat and jumping into the content of the discussion.

You could lead members through an exercise (i.e. cost/benefit or risk analysis) in which they discuss what can go wrong when implementing their proposed solution in hopes that they'll discover the inherent flaws for themselves.

*Offering information in order to help a group make a better decision is **not** overstepping the boundaries of neutrality.*

Staying neutral when you are also an expert

In some situations you not only bring your facilitation skills to the table, but also your expertise in a field related to the group's discussion. This often happens when you're hired as an external facilitator. In these cases the client expects you to offer ideas and make suggestions as well as facilitate.

If there's an expectation that you'll be offering your "expert" advice from time to time, make this clear to the members at the start of the session. It's also good practice to signal when you're speaking as an expert, so people understand when this is happening.

When members facilitate in a small group

Another neutrality dilemma occurs in small "breakout" groups of only three or four people. If one member assumes the facilitator's role, he or she is removed from the discussion, leaving only two or three to make decisions. If the group can't afford to bring in an outside facilitator, the group is in danger of losing valuable ideas from the person playing the neutral role.

There are a number of solutions to this dilemma. First, all of the members, including the facilitator, can write down their ideas before the discussion. The ideas of the facilitator can then be presented by one of the other members during the discussions. Another solution is that the person facilitating can add ideas by asking pointed questions and offering suggestions. Finally, the facilitator can add ideas near the end of each round of discussions by "taking off the facilitator's hat" and temporarily stepping out of the role.

How Assertive Can a Facilitator Be?

Consider this scenario. You're facilitating a meeting in which a key decision has to be made; however, two of the members get embroiled in a conflict. They take turns interrupting one another. Neither one is listening or acknowledging the other. Tempers rise. As the conflict escalates you stand by helplessly saying nothing, in the mistaken belief that staying neutral means "staying totally out of it."

This scenario addresses a common misconception that taking a neutral stance on the *content* of meetings means being "passive." This is far from the truth. In fact, if you operate on the belief that your role is basically unassertive, you'll be in danger of ending up as nothing more than a note taker or scribe, while conflicts rage around you.

While it's true that facilitators should be non-directive on the topic being discussed, they *have to be assertive on the process aspects* of any meeting. It's within the boundaries of the facilitator role to decide all aspects of the meeting process, including informing members how agenda items will be handled, which discussion tools will be used, who will speak in which order and so on.

During discussions, a good facilitator is always assertive in managing member interactions. This involves asking people to rephrase negative comments, calling for breaks and changing the order of items if the flow needs to be adjusted.

New facilitators mistakenly think that they have to be passive during conflicts.

This doesn't mean that you shouldn't collaborate with members on the session design. Gaining members' input is always a good idea; it creates buy-in to both the process design and the challenge the group is being asked to take on. What it does mean is that process is the special expertise of the facilitator. In matters of process it's appropriate for you to have the *final say*.

Just how appropriate and necessary a high level of assertiveness is can be best understood when a group becomes dysfunctional. In these situations you need to be firm and act like a referee, stepping into the fray to restore order to the proceedings.

A high level of assertiveness on process is especially critical whenever there are personal attacks or other rude behavior. All facilitators are empowered to interrupt and redirect individuals so that their interactions become more appropriate. In the section on *Managing Conflict* (Chapter 5), you'll find more on techniques and language you can use for making interventions and managing stormy meetings. By following these practices, you'll be behaving in a way that's anything but passive.

Some assertive actions facilitators take, when the situation warrants it, include:

While facilitators need to be passive on **content,** *they must be active on* **process.**

- informing participants about the design of the session
- insisting on meeting norms
- calling on quiet people
- stopping to check on the process
- calling time outs and breaks
- intervening in order to stop rude behavior
- asking penetrating questions
- challenging people's assumptions
- making changes in the meeting design midstream
- summarizing discussions
- pushing for closure
- insisting that detailed action plans be in place
- implementing evaluation and feedback exercises

Who can facilitate?

Once a group has recognized the need for facilitation, there's often confusion about who the facilitator should be. Should it be:

- the leader of the group?
- a member?
- someone from the outside?

Anyone who regularly attends team or committee meetings should be capable of facilitating.

Because of the relative shortage of skilled facilitators, it's impossible to get external support for every meeting that requires it. It therefore makes more sense to train everyone who attends meetings so they can meet this need.

When to use external resources

An outsider is essential if the discussion to be held requires the full participation of all members. Choosing external facilitators to handle complex issues with large groups (i.e. a senior management retreat) is an excellent strategy.

As an external facilitator you have several advantages:

- you're assumed to be a credible, expert facilitator
- you're above the fray and can walk away afterward
- you're unencumbered by political or emotional baggage
- you can often afford to take more risks
- you don't have to live with the decisions
- you get paid for your efforts as a professional

However, being an external facilitator also offers drawbacks:

- you need to gather basic data since you're unfamiliar with the group or the organization
- you don't know the personalities of the individuals; what to focus on and what to avoid; historical faux pas, etc.
- you need to create rapport and comfort to ensure trust
- you don't get to see the initiatives of the group unfold

When leaders facilitate

Leaders can lead most meetings provided they aren't needed as members. Their facilitation also has to be seen as sufficiently neutral.

If you are the leader/facilitator for your group, you enjoy some real advantages over an external person. By far the most valuable is that you understand the issues and resources of the group in a way that no outside person could. You also:

- know what degree of risk can be taken
- feel comfortable with the members
- know the strengths and weaknesses of individuals

The biggest disadvantage for a leader-as-facilitator is that others may not view you as neutral. In addition:

- you are not automatically given credibility as a facilitator
- you have a rank in the group that can hinder openness
- your role as facilitator may run counter to your traditional leadership style

Leaders who facilitate need to clearly explain their role and deal with neutrality issues at the start of their sessions.

When members facilitate

On the ideal team, all members have highly developed facilitation skills and take turns managing meetings. Like the leader, members will encounter many of the same challenges, such as having to earn credibility and working hard to stay neutral.

Members who facilitate will have to deal with being cast into a leadership position, which may create a power shift within the group. If this poses a problem in your group, the matter will need to be discussed in advance.

Members who facilitate gain important leadership skills.

Facilitation As a Leadership Style

While there's a pressing need for all team leaders to become proficient facilitators, this is often a difficult challenge.

For decades organizations have wanted leaders to have all the answers, take charge and make the tough decisions. The result of this directive style is that many managers are "hooked" on being in control. Under these circumstances, employees are often reluctant to openly express their opinions. There are many groups that are impossible to facilitate if the official leader is in the room. After all, who's going to feel comfortable expressing an opinion if there's even the slightest chance it might contradict what the "boss" thinks? An employee who feels this way will tell you that he or she doesn't want to make decisions and isn't paid enough to be held accountable.

Over the decades, the "control and command" model of leadership has created a culture in which those at the front line are relegated to being doers and totally underutilized as thinkers. This may have worked in the old-fashioned world of assembly lines, but it's a terrible waste of human resources in today's knowledge-driven world.

Every organization needs the intelligence, commitment and energy of *all* its members. This level of engagement can only be fostered by a shift in leadership: from telling to asking, from controlling to facilitating. This change won't happen quickly because so many of us are conditioned by the idea that if someone is up at the front of a room managing a meeting, he or she's "in charge" and ought to make the final decisions. This directive leadership role is in decline today. It's now less acceptable for a leader to do all the talking and for everyone else to just listen.

The fastest way any leader can change his or her directive style is to become facilitative at meetings. Instead of participating in the discussion, leaders can use facilitation to empower and ensure that other people's best ideas are brought out. Of course, this is easier said than done.

The reality is that facilitation promotes a more democratic way of making decisions, which is a major adjustment for some leaders. While there will always be some decisions that should be made by one person (see p. 115 for more on decision-making options), a facilitator's goal is to create consensus on issues.

Managers who adopt facilitation, therefore, have to accept that consensus and majority voting must become the dominant decision-making methods. Shifting one's style to facilitation means learning to live with the decisions of others.

Some managers try to get the best of both worlds by having one of their team members become an expert at facilitation, while they stay in the control mode. While this may seem to work, the leader will ultimately discover that using facilitation makes the group's culture more democratic regardless of who is actually standing at the flip chart.

Managers who are reluctant to facilitate sometimes fear they'll be left with no real role to play. This is a misconception. When a leader facilitates, he or she is needed just as much as before because "process" leadership is such a full and needed job.

We are shifting from manager as order giver, to manager as facilitator.

Using facilitation means learning to live with the decisions of others.

The Power of Facilitation

When leaders shift their paradigm from controlling and directing to facilitating and empowering, they often feel as though they have given up all of their familiar "power tools." In reality, there's a substantial amount of power and control built into the role of facilitator. The difference is that this power is exerted indirectly, through the application of process, rather than through direct control. Consider the following examples of how process can be used to manage and control the activities of a group.

Situation	Old Directive Approach	Facilitative Process Approach
Members misbehave	↦ give them a pep talk about getting along	↦ have members create rules they agree to abide by
A bad decision is made	↦ overturn it, then explain why	↦ have members critique their decision using reality-based criteria
Members overstep their authority	↦ rein them in, supervise more carefully	↦ help clarify specific empowerment levels so that authority is clear

When operating in a group setting, a facilitator actually has much more control than a manager operating without process tools. With process knowledge, a leader can exert tremendous influence. Using a facilitative process approach, leaders can:

- get groups to set and achieve stretch goals
- build and maintain high-performance teams
- run efficient and highly effective meetings
- engage groups in process improvement
- settle conflicts between groups
- systematically solve organizational problems
- manage interpersonal dynamics

Rather than viewing facilitation as a disempowering change, leaders need to see the inherent advantages in being a master of "process."

*Facilitation techniques **give** leaders power in managing groups.*

The Impact of Facilitating

Never underestimate how a shift in leadership paradigm impacts others. When you're a leader who facilitates, staff are forced to stop relying on you for answers and will draw on their own resources. Instead of coming to you with questions, they learn to bring solutions. Instead of complying with orders, they'll participate in creating plans for which they'll have a high level of commitment. When presented with more information, they'll offer more ideas. When given more decision-making authority, they'll weigh options more carefully. Instead of waiting for direction, they'll become engaged in setting the direction.

When you adopt a facilitative approach, each group member becomes a leader, because there is pressure to take initiative. In fact, the hallmark of a good leader is that all of the group's members become leaders themselves. Similarly, the sign of a great facilitator is that all members of the group become skilled facilitators, too.

Facilitation is empowering.

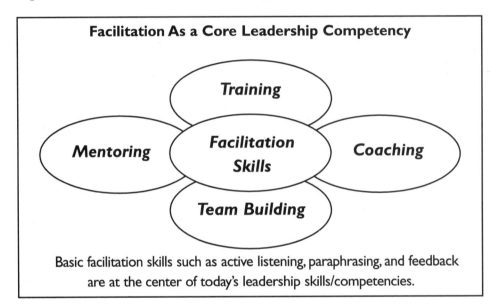

Facilitation As a Core Leadership Competency

Training

Mentoring

Facilitation Skills

Coaching

Team Building

Basic facilitation skills such as active listening, paraphrasing, and feedback are at the center of today's leadership skills/competencies.

Balancing the Roles of Leader and Facilitator

When you're an outside facilitator, you'll often find yourself managing meetings at which the regular leader is also present. This can be a source of power struggles, when it needn't be.

Since there is a clear delineation between *content* and *process* functions, the two roles can easily be kept distinct. Make it clear that the leader will be participating as a member of the group, while as the facilitator, you'll manage how the meeting is run.

Role problems often stem from the fact that the manager doesn't want to be "just a member" of the team. She or he may be used to a more controlling style and may want to dominate both the discussion and also how the meeting should be run.

All experienced facilitators have stories about clients who meddle in *process* designs to the point at which these designs need to be repaired mid-meeting. These repairs often represent a return to the design originally proposed by the facilitator.

Since it's the facilitator who is on the spot when a design doesn't work, leaders and members need to be diplomatically asked to give their ideas and advice, and avoid dictating the actual meeting *process*. This all-too-common dilemma reinforces the need to clarify roles right at the preplanning stage, so that everyone understands that the facilitator has the final say on how the meeting is run.

Many managers use external facilitators because they have difficulty staying neutral. When a manager is domineering, she or he often ends up hampering the active participation of other members.

It's quite appropriate for you to advise a potentially "controlling" manager to temper his or her role. The best way to ensure that there is close cooperation between leader and facilitator is to meet before the session and plan the agenda together. As the facilitator, you need to know what the leader wants to achieve at the session, which items are most important, and how much time is appropriate for each item. There is a more detailed description of strategies for dealing with domineering leaders on page 73.

Clarify roles right at the start.

Best and Worst Facilitator Practices

Some of the best things that a facilitator can do:

→ carefully assess the needs of the members
→ probe sensitively into people's feelings
→ create an open and trusting atmosphere
→ help people understand why they're there
→ view yourself as servant of the group's needs
→ make members the center of attention
→ speak in simple and direct language
→ work hard to stay neutral
→ display energy and appropriate levels of assertiveness
→ champion ideas not personally favored
→ treat all participants as equals
→ stay flexible and ready to change direction if necessary
→ make notes that reflect what participants mean
→ listen intently to understand totally what is being said
→ periodically summarize a complex array of ideas so that they form a coherent summary
→ know how to use a wide range of discussion tools
→ make sure every session ends with clear steps for the next meeting
→ ensure that participants feel ownership for what has been achieved
→ end on a positive and optimistic note

Some of the worst things a facilitator can do:

→ remain oblivious to what the group thinks or needs
→ never check group concerns
→ not listen carefully to what's being said
→ lose track of key ideas
→ take poor flip chart notes or change the meaning of what's said
→ try to be the center of attention
→ get defensive
→ get into personality battles
→ put down people
→ unassertively manage conflict
→ let a few people or the leader dominate
→ never check how the meeting is going
→ be overly passive on process
→ push ahead on an irrelevant agenda
→ have no alternative approaches
→ let discussions get badly sidetracked
→ let discussion ramble without proper closure
→ not know when to stop
→ be insensitive to cultural diversity issues
→ use inappropriate humor

Facilitator Behaviors and Strategies

Regardless of whether you're a facilitator from inside the group or out, the team's leader or a member, the following are parameters for facilitator behaviors.

Be Informed – Successful facilitators always gather extensive data about their prospective participants in order to fully understand both their business and their needs. They survey and interview participants, read background reports and use prepared questions to build a complete picture of the group's situation.

Be Optimistic – Facilitators do not allow disinterest, antagonism, shyness, cynicism or other negative reactions to throw them off. They try instead to focus on what can be achieved and to draw the best from each participant.

Be Consensual – Facilitation is fundamentally a consensus-building process. Facilitators always strive to create outcomes that reflect the ideas of all participants equally.

Be Flexible – Successful facilitators always have a *process* plan for all meetings, yet at the same time should be ready to toss it aside and change direction if that's what is needed. Really great facilitators bring alternative strategies and possess a good command of *process* tools.

Be Understanding – There are great pressures on employees in today's workplace. Facilitators need to understand this and recognize that antagonistic or cynical behaviors are a result of high stress levels.

Be Alert – All great facilitators are expert people watchers. They pay careful attention to group dynamics and notice what is going on at all times. All process leaders need to train themselves to be watchful of both how people interact and how well they are achieving the task.

Be Firm – Good facilitation is not a passive activity. It often takes a substantial level of assertiveness to keep people and activities on track. Facilitators should be ready to step in and direct the process if the situation calls for it.

Be Unobtrusive – The facilitator should do as little talking as possible. The participants should be doing all of the talking. The facilitator says only enough to give instructions, stop arguments, keep things on track and sum up. Trying to be the center of attention or make yourself look important is a misuse of your position.

Special Note:

Facilitating should be an egoless activity. The purpose is to make the group succeed, not to make you look really important and clever. An effective facilitator will leave a group convinced that "We did it ourselves!"

*You can
only learn to
facilitate by
practicing.*

Practice Feedback Sheets

An excellent way of getting better at facilitating is to ask a colleague to observe you in action and then give you feedback. On the next two pages are two different observation sheets for feedback purposes. The first focuses on core practices, while the second emphasizes the elements of *process* requirements during any meeting.

Regardless of which sheet is used, the following feedback process can be helpful:

1. First talk about how you feel you did. Ask "What did you think were your strengths? Weaknesses? What do you think could be improved?"

2. Next, have the observers offer specific descriptions of all the things they noted that you did effectively.

3. Finally, have the observers provide concrete suggestions for improvements that they believe would enhance your facilitation effectiveness.

✎ Notes

_____

_____

_____

_____

_____

_____

_____

_____

_____

_____

_____

Facilitation Core Practices Observation Sheet

Facilitator:	Observer:

Behaviors that Help

___ listens actively

___ maintains eye contact

___ helps identify needs

___ gets buy-in

___ surfaces concerns

___ defines problems

___ brings everyone into the discussion

___ uses good body language and intonation

___ paraphrases continuously

___ provides feedback

___ accepts and uses feedback

___ checks time and pace

___ provides useful feedback

___ monitors and adjusts the process

___ asks relevant, probing questions

___ keeps an open attitude

___ stays neutral

___ offers suggestions

___ is optimistic and positive

___ manages conflict well

___ takes a problem-solving approach

___ stays focused on process

___ ping-pongs ideas around

___ makes accurate notes that reflect the discussion

___ looks calm and pleasant

___ is flexible about changing the approach used

___ skillfully summarizes what is said

___ knows when to stop

Behaviors that Hinder

___ oblivious to group needs

___ no follow-up on concerns

___ poor listening

___ strays into content

___ loses track of key ideas

___ makes poor notes

___ ignores conflicts

___ provides no alternatives for structuring the discussion

___ gets defensive

___ puts down people

___ no paraphrasing

___ lets a few people dominate

___ never asks "How are we doing?"

___ tries to be center of attention

___ lets the group get sidetracked

___ projects a poor image

___ uses negative or sarcastic tone

___ talks too much

___ doesn't know when to stop

Additional Observations:

_____

_____

_____

_____

_____

Facilitation Process Flow Observation Sheet

Facilitator:	Observer's Comments:
Clarifies the purpose	_____
Creates buy-in for the proposed challenge	_____
Checks assumptions	_____
Makes sure there are norms	_____
Establishes the process	_____
Sets time frames	_____
Stays neutral and objective	_____
Paraphrases continuously	_____
Acts lively and positively	_____
Makes clear notes	_____
Asks good probing questions	_____
Makes helpful suggestions	_____
Encourages participation	_____
Addresses conflict	_____
Sets a good pace	_____
Checks the process	_____
Moves smoothly to new topics	_____
Makes clear and timely summaries	_____
Knows when to stop	_____

Facilitation Skill Levels

Mastering the art of neutrality, keeping notes and asking questions at meetings is not all there is to facilitating. Being a true facilitator means developing your competency at four distinct levels.

Review the skills needed at each of the four levels described below. Then complete the facilitation skills and needs assessment instrument that follows to identify your current strengths and future training needs.

Level 1

Understanding concepts, values and beliefs; use of facilitative behaviors such as active listening, paraphrasing, questioning, summarizing; managing time; encouraging participation; keeping clear and accurate notes; using basic tools like problem solving and action planning.

Level 2

Mastering process tools; designing meetings; skilled at using the right decision-making method, achieving consensus and getting true closure; handling feedback activities and conducting process checks; using exit surveys; good at managing meetings in an effective manner; able to help a group set goals and objectives that are measurable; skilled at checking assumptions and challenging ideas.

Level 3

Skilled at managing conflict and making immediate interventions; able to deal with resistance and personal attacks; making design changes on the spot; sizing up a group and using the right strategies for its developmental stage; managing survey feedback exercises; able to design and conduct interviews and focus groups, design and implement surveys; consolidating ideas from a mass of information into coherent summaries.

Level 4

Design and implement process interventions in response to complex organizational issues; use tools to promote process improvement, customer intimacy and overall organizational effectiveness; able to support teams in the various stages of team development.

Facilitation Skills Self-Assessment

Assess your *current* skill levels by rating yourself according to the basic skill areas outlined below.

Rank your *current* skill level using the 4-point scale below.

1	2	3	4
no skill	a little skill	good skill level	totally competent

Level 1   Rating

1. Understand the concepts, values and beliefs of facilitation _____
2. Skilled at active listening, paraphrasing, questioning and summarizing key points _____
3. Able to manage time and maintain a good pace _____
4. Armed with techniques for getting active participation and generating ideas _____
5. Keep clear and accurate notes that reflect what participants have said _____
6. Familiar with the basic tools of systematic problem solving, brainstorming and force-field analysis _____

Level 2

1. Knowledge of a wide range of procedural tools essential for structuring group discussions _____
2. Able to design meetings using a broad set of process tools _____
3. Knowledge of the six main decision-making approaches _____
4. Skilled at achieving consensus and gaining closure _____
5. Skilled at using feedback processes. Able to hear and accept personal feedback _____
6. Able to set goals and objectives that are measurable _____
7. Able to ask good probing questions that challenge own and others' assumptions in a non-threatening way _____
8. Able to stop the action and check on how things are going _____
9. Able to use exit surveys to improve performance _____
10. Able to manage meetings in an orderly and effective manner _____

Level 3

1. Able to manage conflict between participants and remain composed _____
2. Able to make quick and effective interventions _____
3. Able to deal with resistance non-defensively _____
4. Skilled at dealing with personal attacks _____

5. Able to redesign meeting processes on the spot   _____
6. Able to size up a group and use the right strategies for their   _____
   developmental stage
7. Able to implement survey feedback exercises   _____
8. Able to design and conduct interviews and focus groups   _____
9. Knowledgeable about survey design and questionnaire   _____
   development
10. Able to integrate and consolidate ideas from a mass of   _____
    information and create coherent summaries

Level 4

1. Able to design and implement process interventions in   _____
   response to complex organizational issues
2. Able to facilitate process improvement, customer intimacy   _____
   and other organization development activities
3. Able to support teams in their forming, storming and   _____
   performing stages

My current skills (Include all the items you ranked as 4 or 5)

_____

_____

_____

_____

_____

The skills I most need to work on (Choose the ones most
immediately important from all the ones ranked as 1 or 2)

_____

_____

_____

_____

_____

Facilitation at a Glance Chart

To start a facilitation

- welcome participants
- introduce members
- explain your role
- clarify session goal
- ratify agenda
- explain the process
- set time frames
- appoint time keeper
  and minute taker
- start the discussion

Remember to:

- stay neutral
- make eye contact
- include quiet people
- paraphrase actively
- weave their ideas together
- ask probing questions
- park off-topic items
- watch the time
- refer questions back to them

During a facilitation

- ask "*How's this going?*"
- check the pace: too
  fast, too slow?
- check whether the
  techniques are working
- take the pulse of
  members
- summarize periodically
  and at end of session

Manage Conflict by:

1. Venting feelings:
   - listen
   - empathize
   - clarify
2. Resolving the issue:
   take a problem-solving
   approach and end with clear
   action steps

To end a facilitation

- help members make a
  clear statement of
  what was decided
- develop clear next
  steps with dates
  and names
- round up leftover items
- help create next agenda
- clarify follow-up process
- evaluate the session

Tool Kit

Visioning
Sequential Questioning
Brainstorming
Idea Building
Force-Field Analysis
Multi-Voting
Root Cause Analysis
Decision Grids
Troubleshooting
Systematic Problem-Solving

Be Soft on People – Hard on Issues!

Chapter 2
Facilitation Stages

One of the biggest mistakes you can make as a facilitator is to show up at a meeting without having assessed the situation or prepared design notes for the session. Before you facilitate any meeting you should be aware of the specific stages involved to ensure proper planning and implementation.

While the following steps are most often followed by an external facilitator, these steps can also be used if you're an internal person who is asked to plan and run a complex meeting or workshop. Note that steps 4, 5 and 6 are useful in facilitating any small group discussion.

Preparation can be as important as the facilitation itself.

Stages in Conducting a Facilitation
1. Assessment and Design
2. Feedback and Refinement
3. Final Preparation
4. Starting a Facilitation
5. During a Facilitation
6. Ending a Facilitation
7. Following Up on a Facilitation

} Applicable steps for any meeting

1. Assessment and Design

The first step in ensuring success in any facilitation is to make sure the meeting design is based on detailed information about the group.

If you're coming from outside, ask the group's leader to send a letter to all members, informing them that an external facilitator has been brought in and that you will be contacting them to gather background information.

The best way to start is by interviewing the person who asked you to conduct the meeting. In addition to this person, it's important to also gather information from at least a few other members. Always check your, and their, assumptions by gathering data from a cross-section of members. There's nothing worse than basing the design of a meeting on what the leader has told you, only to find that no one else in the group agrees with that assessment. Think of all that wasted time, plus the pressure of adjusting a meeting design on-the-spot.

To assess the needs and status of the group, you can use one or more of the following techniques:

- one-on-one interviews
- group interviews
- surveys
- observations

Samples and details of each technique are included in Chapter 3, starting on page 47.

Any time you gather data about a group, a summary of that information *must* always be fed back to the group. This can be done by providing the members with a written summary of the assessment notes or by writing key points on a flip chart and reviewing them briefly at the start of the session.

If possible, share this feedback before the meeting agenda is presented. If you've done a good job, the design of the meeting should sound like it flows directly from the information gathered.

Once all the data is in and you feel confident that you understand the group and their needs, you can create a preliminary design. This includes identifying the objectives of the session and writing an agenda with detailed process notes. Refer to page 182 for examples of process notes.

Ensure that the members understand the meeting design.

2. Feedback and Refinement

Once you've created a detailed agenda for the session, it's wise to share that design with group members and get their input and approval.

If your design is intended for a large group, or a complex event, this feedback activity will need to be more formal. It's common to meet with a workshop team of two or three group members so that they can hear the feedback from the data gathering and review the proposed design being presented. If the design is for a smaller, less complex meeting, it's fine to discuss your agenda ideas with the leader and/or representative member.

There are many situations in which the groups' members may not like what you've designed. There's often a gap between what a group wants and what the facilitator thinks they need.

Don't back down too easily if you feel the group really needs to discuss certain items.

If a disagreement about the design arises, you need to ensure that all view-points are heard and that optional designs are considered. If the group has valid reasons for not wanting to do an exercise (i.e. the content is too sensitive to discuss, the objectives have changed, etc.), respect that concern.

On the other hand, you should stand firm and assertively promote your design, especially if meeting members are new or reluctant to use participatory techniques or have a history of dysfunction. In these cases listen to their objections, then help them understand your recommendations. Sometimes what they want is not what they need.

Once agreement on a final workshop design has been reached, you can write a brief summary of both the feedback and final version of the design and send it to the group's representatives. This written memo will help reduce the potential for misunderstanding.

3. Final Preparation

Professional facilitators spend as much time preparing for a facilitation session as they do leading the actual event. The industry standard for session leaders is one day of preparation for each day of facilitation. Some complex sessions even have a ratio of two days of preparation for each day of facilitation.

Here are common time allocations for facilitation assignments:

Workshop/ Meeting Length	Interview Time	Design Time	Total Time
1–day workshop (18 people)	1/2 day	1/2 day ➡	2 days
2–day workshop (18 people)	1 day	1 day ➡	4 days
2–day retreat (60 people)	1 day	3 days ➡	6 days

Planning is vitally important.

What should be done as part of final preparation:

__ finalize the design and put it in writing for the client

__ clarify the roles and responsibilities of all parties

__ check the suitability of the meeting location

__ help the group leader prepare a letter detailing meeting logistics and the final agenda

__ identify all materials and supplies required

__ design and write all workshop materials and handouts

__ complete all overheads and required flip charts

The members of the group are typically responsible for sending letters to other members, arranging and paying for all logistics such as meals and accommodations, ensuring that a suitable meeting room is available, arranging and paying for printing, making sure members attend, keeping clear minutes of the proceedings, transcribing all flip chart notes, monitoring to ensure follow-through on all action plans, and evaluating the results.

4. Starting a Facilitation

As the facilitator, you should always be the first person to arrive for any meeting. This ensures that there's time to make last-minute seating changes in the meeting room, post the agenda and survey data, test the equipment, and so on.

Room set-up is critical for sessions. A large room with modular furniture works best for both large group and subgroup settings. Huge boardroom tables, on the other hand, are detrimental to creating an atmosphere conducive to dialogue. A long table also tends to reinforce hierarchical patterns and discourage eye contact between members.

When facilitating large groups it is best that you seat the attendees at round tables spaced evenly around the room. Small table groups consisting of between five to eight persons are ideal.

Make sure there is ample wall space for posting the flip chart sheets that will be generated throughout the day. Lots of easels are usually needed; order one for each subgroup and two for the front of the room.

Chatting informally with members as they arrive not only helps break the ice, it gives people an opportunity to get to know you.

You'll develop your own personal approach for beginning a session over time; however, this one will help you get started:

 ___ introduce yourself and give a brief personal background

___ clarify the role you'll be playing as the facilitator

___ clarify the roles to be played by any other members

___ go around the room and have members introduce themselves by name and perhaps position, especially if there are people present who don't know each other

___ conduct a warm-up activity to relax the group. Make sure this fits with the time available and activity focus

___ review any data collected from members. Have key points written on flip chart paper or on overheads. Answer questions

___ clarify the goal and the specific objectives for the session

___ review the agenda and invite comments. Make any changes

___ specify time frames. Appoint a timekeeper. Make sure there is true acceptance of the agenda

___ take care of all housekeeping items

___ ask the group to set norms for the session; post these on a wall within clear view of all members

___ set up a parking sheet to keep track of digressions for later review

___ proceed to the first item on the agenda. Make sure everyone is clear about what's about to be discussed

___ explain the *process*, or how you'll be handling this agenda item

___ be sure that the time frame for the first item is set. Have a timekeeper and a minute taker on hand

___ get on with the discussion

Be the first to arrive and pay attention to room set-up.

5. During a Facilitation

Your key contribution during any meeting is to provide the structure and process focus that will keep the discussion moving efficiently and effectively. You'll need to:

__ ensure that all members participate
__ manage conflicts
__ keep the group on topic
__ "park" off-topic items
__ help members adhere to their ground rules
__ make interventions if there are problems
__ maintain a high energy level
__ set a positive tone
__ keep track of the discussion by making concise notes

As a meeting proceeds, periodically employ the following process checks:

Constantly monitor how the discussion is going. Use "process checks" to stay on course.

Check the pace — ask members how the pace feels to them
> *"Is this session dragging or do you feeling rushed? What can we do to improve the pace?"*
Respond to their assessments by implementing needed adjustments.

Check the process — periodically ask members if the approach being taken is working
> *"We said we would work this issue through as a large group, rather than sub-grouping. Is this approach working or should we try something else?"*
Adjust the process throughout the session to ensure that things keep working.

Take the pulse of members — continuously read faces and body language to determine how people are feeling. Don't hesitate to ask
> *"How are members feeling? Do we need a stretch? Is anyone feeling like they've dropped out? How can we get our energy levels up again?"*
"Reading" people lets you know when to stop for a break or bring lost members back into the fold.

Summarize — when there are lots of the ideas floating, summarize what's being said. Stop and review:
> *"Let's see what we've got so far."*
If the discussion seems to be winding up:
> *"Let me read what we've said to see if we've reached a conclusion."*
Summarizing helps people who might have lost track of the conversation get back in. It can revive a group in a slump or help move the group toward closure.

6. Ending a Facilitation

One of the most common problems in any meeting is lack of closure. Lots of things get discussed, but there is no clear path forward. One of your key contributions is to ensure that decisions are arrived at and detailed action steps are in place before the group adjourns.

Here are some ways you can help a group bring effective closure to a meeting:

__ make clear statements about what has been decided and write these decisions on a flip chart

__ ensure that they've created detailed action plans with names, accountabilities and dates beside each step

__ round up items not discussed at the meeting, including those on the "parking lot" list, prioritize them, and create plans to deal with them in future

__ create an agenda for the next meeting

__ decide on a means for follow-up, either written reports or a group session

__ help members decide who will take all the flip chart sheets for transcribing

__ conduct a written evaluation of the session

__ solicit personal feedback from participants

__ allow members to express how they felt about the session

__ clarify your role in the follow-up process

Once the session is over, thank the participants for having you facilitate and help clean up.

7. Following Up on a Facilitation

No matter how formal or informal the facilitation process has been, follow-up with the group is always a good idea. If the facilitation consisted of a brief meeting, you might simply call the group leader to determine the extent to which the session helped the group become more effective.

If the session was a major decision-making workshop or retreat, encourage the group leader to send out a written follow-up questionnaire to the members.

Unless it was formally agreed that you would conduct the follow-up activity, you can leave any post-session reports to the group's members. This ensures that they, not you, assume accountability for the implementation of the ideas emerging from the session. Your role may be to merely remind the group about the need for follow-up and to provide them with a format for reporting results later.

In some cases you may negotiate with the group to facilitate a follow-up meeting at which the progress is discussed and evaluated.

There is nothing worse than a discussion that never gets to a decision point.

After a facilitation, you may wish to formally follow up with the members to determine if the session was a success.

 Sample Follow-Up Report Format

Please provide your feedback and update information about our session.

Date: ————————————

Objective: ———————————————————————

Results achieved: What do you regard as the major outcomes of the meeting?

Work completed: Which of the action plans created at the session has been completed by you since then? What was achieved?

Work outstanding: Which action items are you still working on or planning to work on? What's the time frame for these activities?

Next steps: Are there any steps that the whole group needs to take in order to help you complete your action plans? Are there any further discussions that need to take place?

✎ *Notes*

_____

_____

_____

_____

_____

_____

_____

_____

_____

_____

_____

_____

_____

_____

_____

_____

_____

_____

_____

_____

_____

_____

Chapter 3
Knowing Your Participants

Getting to know the people you'll be working with is an essential first step in designing effective meetings. Before you facilitate you need to know if they are:

___ total strangers who have never met before and won't be together again after this single special-purpose meeting

___ total strangers or people who have only a passing acquaintance with each other, but who will be working together again after this meeting

___ a group of people who know each other, have interacted for some time and get along well

___ a group in turmoil who meet periodically and either spin their wheels in frustration or get embroiled in conflicts that are rarely resolved

___ a high-performance team with a solid track record of achievements, made up of members with highly developed people skills who are good at managing group dynamics

Always take the time to get to know your participants.

Conducting an Assessment

Never take a group or situation for granted. Different situations require distinct activities. It's up to you to carefully read a group and design a process that matches their circumstances.

So, how do you get the information you need? Try one of these approaches:

- ***One-on-one interviews*** allow you to question people about the state of the team and member interactions. This is the best way to get people to open up and be candid when there are sensitive issues in the group.

- ***Group interviews or focus groups*** are a good strategy when the subject isn't overly sensitive and/or there are too many people to interview singly. Group interviews let you observe the group's interpersonal dynamics before the actual facilitation session.

- ***Surveys*** let you gather anonymous information from all members. They enable you to compile answers to the same questions from each member. They also generate quantifiable data.

- ***Observing the group in action*** helps you understand the interpersonal dynamics. This involves sitting on the sidelines during meetings in order to get a sense of who plays which roles and how people relate to each other. It's very useful if the team is in conflict.

Assessment Questions

When meeting a new group, you'll need to ask certain questions to determine the state of the group.

- What's the history of the group?

- How familiar are members with each other?

- Are there clear goals?

- Are there team norms or rules?

- Does everyone participate or do a few dominate?

- To what extent are members honest and open?

- Do members listen to and support each other's ideas?

- How does the group handle any conflicts?

- How are important decisions made?

- Do people leave meetings feeling like something has been achieved?

- How would you describe the group atmosphere?

- Are meetings thoroughly planned and structured or are they basically freewheeling?

- Does the group ever stop to evaluate how it's doing and make corrections?

- What's the best thing about the group? What's the worst?

- How do people feel about being part of this group?

- Describe a recent incident that illustrates how members typically interact.

- Are there any reasons why members might not be open and say what they really think?

- Why do you need (external) facilitation support? Is there any opposition to this?

- What's the worst thing that could happen at this meeting? What could be done to ensure that this doesn't happen?

These questions are presented in survey form on the next page.

Group Assessment Survey

1. How familiar are members of this group with each other?

1	2	3	4
Passing acquaintances	We work together	We're a team	We are a high-performance team

2. Are there clear goals for the group?

1	2	3	4
We have no stated goals	Not sure about the goals	Fairly sure about the goals	Clear goals we set ourselves and monitor

3. Does the group have a clear set of rules to manage interactions?

1	2	3
No rules exist	There are norms but they aren't used effectively	We have and use rules that we created

4. Describe the typical participation pattern.

1	2	3
A few people dominate consistently	Participation varies from topic to topic	Everyone plays an equal role

5. How much honesty and openness is there in this group?

1	2	3	4
People hide what they really think	We are somewhat open	We are quite open	We are totally open and honest

6. How good are members at listening, supporting and encouraging each other?

1	2	3	4
We don't do this at all	We try but don't always succeed	We are fairly skilled at this	We are consistently excellent

7. How do members typically handle differences of opinion?

1	2	3
We get emotional and often argue	Half and half	We always debate objectively and respectfully

Group Assessment Survey, cont'd

8. How are important decisions usually made?

1	2	3	4
One person decides	Vote	Seek compromise	Work together to reach consensus

9. Does the group usually end its meetings with a sense of achievement and clear action plans?

1	2	3	4	5
Never	Rarely	Sometimes	Usually	Always

10. How would you describe the atmosphere between members?

1	2	3	4
Hostile and tense	Satisfactory		Totally relaxed and harmonious

11. How would you describe the group's meetings?

1	2	3	4
Unstructured, a waste of time	So-so		Well planned and productive

12. Does the group ever stop and evaluate how it's doing, and then take action to improve?

1	2	3	4
Never	Rarely	Sporadically	Consistently

Note: See page 193 for instructions on conducting a survey feedback exercise.

Comparing Groups to Teams

In order to design appropriate meeting processes, it's important for you to be aware of the differences between groups and teams, as well as the significant differences between teams at the forming, storming, norming and performing stages of their development.

What Is a Group?

A group is a collection of people who come together to communicate, tackle a problem or coordinate an event. They're a group and not a team because they're missing a number of key ingredients present in any true team. These missing ingredients include:

- a common goal that members view as more important than their individual goals
- clear rules or norms created and used by the team to manage interpersonal relations
- clear roles and responsibilities so that members all know how they're linked
- clear accountabilities so that everyone understands who is responsible for what
- a clear empowerment plan that emphasizes continuous increases in areas of self-management
- a method for frequently evaluating how team members are doing and a method for giving and receiving feedback so that the team can constantly improve

In a group, members usually pursue their own individual purpose. For this reason, group members tend to exhibit "I"-centered behavior when debating. This generally makes a group more competitive and argumentative than a true team. When each person strives to get what's best for him or herself, conflict tends to be handled in a more adversarial manner.

Another major difference is that group members usually don't have linked roles and relationships outside of the group's meetings. Members typically have separate job descriptions and only come together to share information and make decisions that affect them all.

How Is a Team Different?

In contrast to a group, a team is a collection of people who come together to achieve a clear and compelling common goal that they have participated in defining. To the members of a true team, that goal is more important than their own individual pursuits. It's this factor that gives a team its cohesion.

A team also creates a set of norms or rules of conduct that define the team's culture. While a group may be run by a chairman, according to "parliamentary rules of order," a team runs itself by norms created by the members.

While all trout are fish, not all fish are trout! Likewise, all teams are groups, but not all groups are teams.

It's important to know whether you're facilitating a team or just a group.

Team members also cooperate on work planning and coordinate roles. Their work lives are linked together and they depend on each other.

When team members have differences of opinion they tend to debate the ideas rather than argue points of view. They aren't out to gain personal victory, but to arrive at the best solution for the good of the whole team.

While the members of a group generally have only the level of authority inherent in their position within the organization, teams seek and attain higher levels of empowerment. Drawing on each other to make better decisions, a team often evolves toward greater autonomy in managing its work.

There is a definite sequence of stages a team goes through in order to ultimately reach high-performance levels. A group does not tend to follow this pattern. One reason is that team membership is permanent. While a group can operate with members coming and going, the members of a team need to be more consistent. In fact, if a member leaves a team, it may need to briefly return to the forming stage in order to integrate its new member.

Whether teams are created to stay together for a year or indefinitely, they tend to develop more trust and openness than most groups do. Members have bought into the idea of working together and have made a commitment to common action. This helps create the comfort that many people need before they can freely express their ideas and concerns.

A Group	A Team
Individual "I" focus	Collective "We" focus
Individual purpose	Common goal
Operate by external rules of order	Operate by own set of team norms
Operate alone	Have linked roles and responsibilities
Individuals have position authority	Teams seek and gain empowerment
Meet irregularly	Meet regularly
Focus on information sharing and coordinating	Focus on problem solving and process improvement
Have a fixed chairperson	Share leadership role
Fight to be right	Debate to make sound decisions
Are closed	Open and trusting
May like each other	Share a strong bond

Do All Groups Need to Become Teams?

The simple answer is no. While teams have some distinct advantages over groups, not all groups should be developed into teams. A group should stay a group if:

- the members will only be together for a short time
- it's only supposed to do one simple task
- its purpose is solely to share information
- different members come to every meeting
- there's no regular or frequent pattern of meetings
- there's no real need for linked roles or a compelling common goal
- all of the work is best planned and managed by isolated individuals
- there's no intent to empower
- there's no support for teamwork in the organization
- leadership styles are controlling and directive

Conversely, it's distinctly advantageous to do team building with any group if:

- there's a need to create a high level of cohesion and commitment to a common goal
- there's an ongoing task for the group to accomplish
- a consistent set of people will be working closely over an extended period
- members need to link and coordinate their roles closely
- higher empowerment levels will result in improved effectiveness and performance

As a facilitator, you should be aware that you'll probably work with more unstructured groups than real teams who have been through a team-building process. This is one of the factors that makes facilitation a challenge, since unschooled groups are likely to be unstructured, more argumentative and less skilled at effective interpersonal behaviors.

In assignments with untrained groups, you'll find that you often need to conduct team-building activities just to get the group to the point where it can be effective!

Getting a Group to Act Like a Team

Even when a group isn't destined to become a team, it's a good idea to take some tips from rudimentary team building, and get members to at least act like a team while they're working together.

This can be achieved by incorporating a variety of key team-building activities right into the agenda. These activities include:

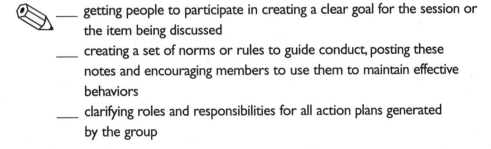

_____ getting people to participate in creating a clear goal for the session or the item being discussed

_____ creating a set of norms or rules to guide conduct, posting these notes and encouraging members to use them to maintain effective behaviors

_____ clarifying roles and responsibilities for all action plans generated by the group

____ clarifying all accountabilities to ensure that everyone is clear about expected results

____ training members in effective team behaviors: how to handle conflict, make decisions, eliminate dysfunctional behavior, etc.

____ conducting process checks, building in feedback loops and other evaluation mechanisms so that members can take responsibility for improving how the group functions at meetings

Understanding Team Stages

If you're working with a true team you need to realize that teams develop through four stages. Each of these stages has unique characteristics and must be facilitated differently.

Forming

Forming is the first stage of team development. It starts when members are first brought together to achieve a specific goal. In the forming stage members tend to be optimistic and expectations are usually high. At the same time there's also some understandable anxiety about fitting in and being able to achieve the task. Despite these early anxieties, forming is generally a "honeymoon" for most teams.

Members of forming teams are usually shy. They hold back until they know each other better. People are guarded with their comments. No one is sure exactly how he or she fits into the new team.

This stage is also characterized by an overdependence on the leader. Members want to be given a clear mandate, structure and parameters.

Forming can last anywhere from a few weeks to several months, depending on how often the team meets and how quickly the team completes the "team formation" agenda.

Facilitating the Formation of a Team

When facilitating a new team, you need to be especially friendly, open and optimistic to help ease everyone's anxieties. Here are some things you can do:

____ make sure there's clarity about the mandate and parameters for the new team

____ help the members collaborate to create a goal that achieves the stated mandate

____ break the ice with activities that create comfort and disclosure

____ be encouraging and empowering

____ help members develop norms or rules of conduct

____ identify tasks and specify roles and responsibilities

____ provide structure for meetings

____ manage participation so that everyone has an equal say

____ set a tone of openness and trust

____ provide training in decision making and effective behaviors

Forming teams require lots of structure.

Creating Team Norms

A major difference between groups and teams is that teams have clear norms or rules set by the team's members. These rules are used by the members to control their own and their peers' behaviors.

Developing norms is essential at the forming stage. Once they're in place, the norms are posted, referred to when behaviors become less than desirable and amended as the team matures.

Norms are always developed by team members. It only makes sense that bringing in norms from outside and asking the members to adhere to them will be largely ineffective. Members will be more likely to follow rules that they've created together.

Norms will vary somewhat with each team, but these are some of the most common:

- We will listen actively to all ideas
- Everyone's opinions count
- No interrupting while someone is talking
- Anyone can call "time out" if he or she feels we need a break
- We will be open, yet honor privacy
- All team discussions will remain confidential
- We will respect differences
- We will be supportive rather than judgmental
- We will give helpful feedback directly and openly
- All team members will offer their ideas and resources
- Each member will take responsibility for the work of the team
- We will respect team meeting times by starting on time, returning from other meetings promptly, avoiding unnecessary interruptions
- We will stay focused on our goals and avoid getting sidetracked
- When we have a difference of opinion we'll debate the facts of the situation and not personalities
- We will all work to make sure there are no hidden agendas, and that all issues and concerns can be dealt with openly by all members

People are more likely to buy in to norms that they have created together.

Storming

Storming is a normal and expected stage of team development. In this stage, members experience a discrepancy between their initial hopes for the team and the realities of working together. Conflict arises and everyone knows that the "honeymoon" is over. Storming can take place for a variety of reasons, including:

Interpersonal conflict: People discover that they like some members, but dislike others. Cliques can form. Two people can start to clash over ideas or personal styles. Some people may not be pulling their weight. Others may talk too much or try to dominate.

Lack of skills: There may be little listening and encouragement among team members due to a lack of training in interpersonal skills. Members may be unfa-

Storming teams need to be facilitated assertively.

miliar with how to manage differences of opinion, so that potential debates end as fights. People often lack skills in such things as problem analysis, how to control a meeting, or giving and receiving feedback. As a result, they're basically unable to manage the team dynamics.

Ineffective leadership: The team leader may be too controlling while the members are trying to flex their muscles. Conversely, the leader may be too laissez faire on certain topics. Members may not like how the leader runs the meetings, or offers his or her assistance. Sometimes leaders have low personal credibility, poor interpersonal skills or are dishonest in their dealings with the team.

Problems with the task: This task may be too difficult for the team. Work loads may be unrealistic. Members often resist taking on more power and responsibility. The task itself may be unclear or the members may not have bought into the task.

Problems with organizational barriers: If the management team doesn't adequately support team empowerment by removing barriers, the team will become frustrated and angry with the system.

During the storming phase it's common for members to feel dissatisfied with their dependence on someone else's authority, most often the team leader's. It's not unusual for members to challenge or even reject the leader at this stage. Power struggles can also take place among members who may be competing for authority.

Because interpersonal squabbles and conflict distract the team from focusing on its main tasks, productivity usually plummets during storming. There's a feeling of ineffectiveness, and meetings where little is decided. Frustration increases. With this comes a corresponding decline in morale. People start to wonder if the team is a good idea, since so much time seems to be wasted.

If you find yourself facilitating a team in storming, be careful not to take this personally. Check to see if this is what you're thinking:

> *This is awful. Things are falling apart!*
> *They hate me! I hate them!*
> *I can't trust them!*
> *Who do they think they are?*
> *I'll fix them!*

In order to survive storming, you need to adopt a more positive mind-set. This includes believing:

> *Storming is OK. It's a normal stage.*
> *They don't hate me; they're just storming.*
> *They don't hate each other; they're just storming.*
> *This is energy I've got to channel into solutions.*
> *We'll get through this together.*

Storming teams pose the greatest facilitation challenges.

Signs of Storming

Use the following checklist to raise your awareness of storming. It can help you determine whether the team you're about to work with is in this sensitive state.

____ there's a tendency toward arguing viewpoints instead of debating ideas

____ people don't listen actively or support each other's ideas

____ the team is divided into factions

____ members vie for power with and against each other

____ members confront the leader in an overly emotional way

____ meetings go in circles; little is achieved

____ members talk about each other outside of meetings

____ there's a tendency to complain, and "Yeah but" most ideas

____ people don't like coming to the meetings. They're often late, absent or don't do their homework

____ no one wants to take responsibility, follow-through is poor

____ some people start to "clam up"; they no longer participate

____ members go to each other after meetings to air their concerns about the team

____ the team isn't achieving its work goals

____ there's no attention to "process" or how the team functions

____ interpersonal aspects overshadow getting the job done

____ people say the team makes them feel drained of energy

____ people no longer think the team is a good idea

Accept that tension is normal in Storming.

Facilitating a Team in Storming

Storming is the most difficult stage to facilitate because feelings are running high. You need to handle the situation carefully in order to remain absolutely neutral, and not take sides in any debates. Storming also demands a high degree of assertiveness on your part. So, how do you cope?

• expect and accept tension as normal
• stay totally neutral and calm
• create an environment in which people can safely express feelings
• honestly and openly admit that there's conflict
• help members identify issues and solve them together
• invite input and feedback
• make interventions to correct dysfunctional behaviors
• assertively referee heated discussions
• train members in group skills
• facilitate communication

When a Team Storms

As a facilitator there are always two approaches for every situation:

BEST ACTIONS	WORST ACTIONS
→ Surface all problems to get them on the table to be solved	→ Ignore problems
→ Create norms that make it safe to discuss problems. Encourage members to debate ideas in a non-personal way	→ Avoid all arguments
→ Offer clear options and encourage members to take control	→ Take back control
→ Help members identify strategies and action plans	→ Tell people what to do
→ Help members identify their problems and resolve them	→ Take a punitive attitude

Norming

You exit storming and enter the norming phase when you stop members and ask them to assess how they're doing as a team, with the intent of seeking solutions to improve the team's operation.

While norming is usually described as a team stage, it's actually a transitional step that moves a team from storming into performing. In norming, the team confronts its problems and resolves them. The resolutions that everyone agrees to become the new norms for the team.

During norming, members face their issues, accept feedback and act on it. This results in improvement in the team's performance.

There are four main norming techniques you can use:

___ ***Survey Feedback:*** Hand out the appropriate survey for the problem your group is experiencing: conflict management, team effectiveness, meeting effectiveness. Feed results back to members for their analysis. Help them identify problems and generate solutions.

___ ***Force-Field Analysis:*** Facilitate a discussion in which members analyze what's working on the team and what's not. Generate solutions for each item identified as not working.

___ ***Personal Feedback:*** Help members give each other personal feedback about what they're doing that is effective and what they could do better.

___ ***Setting New Norms:*** Help members review their existing norms and make the additions needed to manage the current conflict situation.

The Facilitator's Role in Norming

If you're facilitating a group in storming, you need to instigate norming by providing methods for giving and receiving feedback. In norming it's essential that you be totally neutral and focus on managing process. Key facilitator strategies include:

- encouraging problem identification and problem solving
- inviting input and feedback
- offering training and support to team members
- supporting members while they make improvements
- further sharing of power
- mediating in personality clashes
- coaching and counseling individuals
- encouraging others to take on leadership roles

Performing — The Final Team Growth Stage

If norming is managed successfully, the team should enter into a period of improved performance. By this stage, conflicts have been resolved and members will be ready to focus on their work without distraction. Everyone wins here. Productivity goes up. So does morale. In high-performing teams:

- everyone shares power by rotating leadership roles
- the official leader is treated as a valued member
- everyone behaves in a supportive way
- all members take turns facilitating
- the team evaluates and corrects continuously
- members feel committed and bonded
- decisions made are typically high-quality
- time and resources are used efficiently
- conflicts are seen as constructive debates, rarely getting heated or emotional

All *performing* teams have:

1. A clear team goal that has been created by the team and that dovetails with organizational targets
2. Established ground rules or norms that are adjusted regularly and used to monitor and improve the team
3. Detailed work plans that define tasks, clarify roles and responsibilities, lay out a schedule of events and specify the performance expectations of the team
4. Clearly defined empowerment so that members know which decisions they can make
5. Clear and open communication between members and with those outside the team
6. Well-defined decision-making procedures that help the team know which decision-making approach to use
7. Beneficial team behaviors that reflect good interpersonal skills and positive intent to make the team successful
8. Balanced participation so that everyone is heard and the team's decision making isn't dominated by one or two strong personalities

Norming is a "transitional" activity more than a stage.

9. Awareness of group process along with regular initiatives to improve how the team functions

10. Well-planned and executed meetings with detailed agendas

Facilitating a Performing Team

You'll find that the easiest group to facilitate is a high-performance team whose members have learned to manage their own conflict and who have highly developed interpersonal skills. But that doesn't mean your job's over yet. In these situations you need to:

___ collaborate with members on meeting designs to get their input

___ share facilitation duties

___ offer expertise to the team

___ help the team reward and celebrate success

___ offer to observe and give feedback to further improve the team

High-performing teams are the easiest to facilitate.

Facilitation Strategies Chart

Use the following quick reference to match appropriate facilitator approaches with the team-development stage being experienced by the group or team.

Stage	Key Elements	Facilitator Strategies
Group	May be strangers	Warm-up exercises
	"I"-focused individuals	Build buy-in
	Lack of compelling goal	Create a common goal
	No norms	Create and use norms
	Roles loosely linked	Clarify and link roles
	Individual accountabilities	Define accountabilities
		Teach interpersonal skills
		Provide clear process
		Encourage participation
		Evaluate meeting effectiveness

Main Strategy – To provide structure and support

Stage	Key Elements	Facilitator Strategies
Forming	Members unsure	Warm-up exercises
	Uncertainty	Disclosure exercises
	Low trust	Build buy-in
	Need direction	Create a common goal
	Commitment low	Create and use norms
	Group skills unrefined	Define accountabilities
	Overdependence on leader	Clarify roles and responsibilities
		Provide clear process
		Encourage participation
		Evaluate team effectiveness

Main Strategy – Build team spirit and comfort while providing lots of structure for activities

Stage	Key Elements	Facilitator Strategies
Storming	Conflict emerges Frustration sets in Animosities develop Cliques form Leader is rejected Power struggles Emotional arguing	Expect and accept tension Stay neutral and calm Create safety for expressing feelings Honestly admit there's conflict Help members identify and solve issues Invite input and feedback Make interventions Assertively referee conflict Teach interpersonal and conflict management skills Encourage communication

Main Strategy – To listen, address conflict, referee assertively, and resolve issues collaboratively

Stage	Key Elements	Facilitator Strategies
Norming	Members "own" problems Conflicts are resolved Power issues are resolved Team redefines its norms Performance problems corrected Create empowerment plans	Offer methods for feedback Help solve problems Invite personal feedback Offer further training Support members while they make improvements Share power Mediate personality clashes Coach and counsel individuals Share the leadership role

Main Strategy — To support team improvement efforts and encourage member empowerment

Stage	Key Elements	Facilitator Strategies
Performing	High productivity Conflicts managed by members Commitment to goal high Roles and responsibilities clear Members behave in a facilitative manner Team continuously improves itself Members feel committed and bonded	Collaborate with members on process Rotate facilitation duties Offer your expertise Help the team recognize and celebrate success

Main Strategy — build agendas together, share facilitation responsibilities, collaborate, act as a resource

Using Surveys to Improve Performance

If you're asked to facilitate a session aimed at improving a team's performance, the following survey may be useful. The step-by-step survey feedback methodology is described on page 193 in Chapter 9 of this book.

 Team Effectiveness Survey

Instructions: Please give your candid opinion of this team by rating its characteristics on the seven-point scale shown below. Circle the appropriate number on each scale to represent your evaluation. Do not put your name on this. Return the survey in the envelope provided. (Remember, you are rating your immediate work team.)

1. Goal Clarity

Are goals and objectives clearly understood and accepted by all members?

1	2	3	4	5	6	7

Goals and objectives aren't
known, understood or accepted
Goals and objectives are
clear and accepted

2. Participation

Is everyone involved and heard during group discussions or is there a "tyranny of a minority"?

1	2	3	4	5	6	7

A few people tend to dominate
Everyone is active and has a say

3. Consultation

Are team members consulted on matters concerning them?

1	2	3	4	5	6	7

We are seldom consulted
Team members are always consulted

4. Decision Making

Is the group both objective and effective at making decisions?

1	2	3	4	5	6	7

The team is ineffective at
reaching decisions
The team is very effective
at reaching decisions

5. Roles and Responsibilities

When action is planned, are clear assignments made and accepted?

1	2	3	4	5	6	7

Roles are poorly defined
Roles are clearly defined

Chapter 3 - Knowing Your Participants

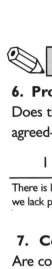 **Team Effectiveness Survey, cont'd**

6. Procedures

Does the team have clear rules, methods and procedures to guide it? Are there agreed-upon methods for problem solving?

| 1 | 2 | 3 | 4 | 5 | 6 | 7 |

There is little structure and we lack procedures

The team has clear rules and procedures

7. Communications

Are communications between members open and honest? Do members listen actively?

| 1 | 2 | 3 | 4 | 5 | 6 | 7 |

Communications are not open
Not enough listening

Communications are open
People listen

8. Confronting Difficulties

Are difficult or uncomfortable issues openly worked through or are conflicts avoided? Are conflicts worked through?

| 1 | 2 | 3 | 4 | 5 | 6 | 7 |

Difficulties are avoided
Little direct conflict management

Problems are attacked
openly and directly

9. Openness & Trust

Are team members open in their transactions? Are there hidden agendas? Do members feel free to be candid?

| 1 | 2 | 3 | 4 | 5 | 6 | 7 |

Individuals are guarded
and hide motives

Everyone is open and
speaks freely

10. Commitment

How committed are team members to deadlines, meetings and other team activities?

| 1 | 2 | 3 | 4 | 5 | 6 | 7 |

Deadlines and commitments
often missed

Total commitment

✎ **Team Effectiveness Survey, cont'd**

11. Support

Do members pull for each other? What happens when one person makes a mistake? Do members help each other?

| 1 | 2 | 3 | 4 | 5 | 6 | 7 |

Little evidence of support   Lots of support

12. Risk Taking

Do individuals feel that they can try new things, risk failure? Does the team encourage risk?

| 1 | 2 | 3 | 4 | 5 | 6 | 7 |

Little support for risk   Lots of support for risk

13. Atmosphere

Is the team atmosphere informal, comfortable and relaxed?

| 1 | 2 | 3 | 4 | 5 | 6 | 7 |

The team spirit is tense   The team is comfortable and relaxed

14. Leadership

Are leadership roles shared, or do the same people dominate and control?

| 1 | 2 | 3 | 4 | 5 | 6 | 7 |

A few people dominate   Leadership is evenly shared

15. Evaluation

Does the team routinely stop and evaluate how it's doing in order to improve?

| 1 | 2 | 3 | 4 | 5 | 6 | 7 |

We never evaluate   We routinely evaluate

16. Meetings

Are meetings orderly, well planned and productive?

| 1 | 2 | 3 | 4 | 5 | 6 | 7 |

Waste of time   Couldn't be better

17. Fun

Is there an "esprit de corps," or sense of fun, on this team?

| 1 | 2 | 3 | 4 | 5 | 6 | 7 |

Humbug!   We have fun!

Clarifying Empowerment Levels

One of the buzzwords that has caused tremendous confusion is the notion of "empowerment." Too often empowerment is poorly defined, and team members are totally confused about the exact extent of their decision-making power.

When a group or team creates action plans, its members must be totally clear about just how much empowerment they have in order to implement each action item successfully. As their facilitator, you need to understand the four levels of empowerment so that you can help members be clear on which level they're operating with each action item.

Empowerment doesn't have to be a vague motion when you use the four-level empowerment model.

Empowerment needn't be confusing!

The Empowerment Continuum

Management Control		**Employee Control**	
I	**II**	**III**	**IV**
Management Decides, Then Informs Staff	**Management Gets Staff Input Before Deciding**	**Employees Decide & Recommend**	**Employees Decide & Act**
• Telling	• Selling	• Participating	• Delegating
• Directing	• Coaching	• Facilitating	• Liaising
• Management is accountable and responsible	• Employees' ideas harnessed as input to decisions	• Accountabilities are clearly shared	• Employees are accountable and responsible
• Management is in control	• Team members are consulted and have input into decisions	• Team members must consult management before acting to get approval	• Team members can set direction and take action without approvals
• Team members are told about decisions			

Here's what the four levels mean:

Level I – this level of decision making is made solely by management. Employees are informed about the decision after it's been made. A memo announcing a change is an example of a level I decision.

Level II – this is a decision made by management after input is obtained from employees. An employee focus group is an example of a level II practice.

Level III – this type of decision involves employees discussing and deciding on a course of action, but unable to act until they receive approval. Problem-solving workshops are often set up as level III activities.

Level IV – this type of decision refers to situations in which the group has been given the authority to make decisions and implement action plans without having to seek final approval. This authority is given to a group on the assumption that the group is willing and able to handle the outcomes.

It's your job as the facilitator to help group members understand and negotiate the exact limits of their power for each situation or activity. It's common for groups to assume they have level IV authority to go ahead, when management assumes they're at level III.

To clarify empowerment levels you need to ask participants:

- *What level of empowerment is appropriate to conduct this activity efficiently?*
- *What level do you assume you already have?*
- *Does the empowerment level need to be checked or negotiated with others? (i.e. team sponsor, management, key stakeholders, etc.)*

Getting Groups to Accept Empowerment Beyond Level III

As the facilitator, you should always be prepared for resistance to taking responsibility for implementing action plans.

Group members' reluctance to take on work may have a number of roots:

- some members aren't used to being empowered and are afraid to take more accountability or risks
- there may be feelings that the actions planned by the group are somehow outside established job descriptions
- there may be a lack of confidence or skill on the part of some participants
- some ideas may arrive at the action stage without real support or commitment from all members
- there may be (a legitimate) concern that the organization isn't going to support the group's initiatives

Unlike managers, who have the authority to "order" reluctant employees to take on new tasks, facilitators have to rely on their process skills to encourage people to overcome resistance.

When you encounter resistance to empowerment within a group, try these steps:

Step 1: *Acknowledge the resistance* – don't ignore or deny it
"I can tell by your reaction that you don't want to take on the job of preparing the budget."

Step 2: *Ask members to explain their reluctance* – let them vent their fears and concerns
"Tell me why you think this assignment will pose problems for you?"

Step 3: *Empathize with the group's situation* – sympathize without agreeing
"I can understand your concern about taking on something so important that is relatively unknown to you."

Step 4: *Ask them to identify strategies for overcoming the resistance they are feeling* – ask
"Under what conditions would you consider taking this assignment on? What assurances, training and support would make you feel you'd be willing to give it a try?"

Step 5: *Facilitate a discussion of their proposed strategies* – while you can offer suggestions, work with their ideas as much as possible. At the end summarize what they said
"So you're saying that if you had some training and someone to double-check your numbers you would be willing to give this a try? Let's talk about what sort of training, when and how long."

> *You can't force groups to accept more empowerment.*

If any group member asks for something unreasonable, like "I'll take this on if my pay is doubled," don't be afraid to say "I'd like to do that but I can't." Encourage him/her to find other strategies to overcome barriers.

The aim of this technique is to get the reluctant members to create strategies for overcoming the barriers themselves. At the end of this process, the team members should feel that they have devised their own plan for becoming more empowered.

Does it always work? The truth is that nothing works in every situation. This technique is, however, the only process-oriented approach available for supporting members to become more empowered. If it fails to work, your only option is to refer the problems to a manager, who may simply "order" the members to take on these new tasks.

Be aware that bringing in an authority figure to order members to take on more responsibility will most likely regress the group's maturity backward to a dependent state of obedience. Since this is undesirable, to say the least, facilitators should try the process approach first.

Special Note: *Always consider the possibility that all or some members chosen for a task may indeed be inappropriate. If this is the case, it's a good idea to review the member list or revise the task to better suit existing members.*

Helping Groups Negotiate Increased Empowerment

Facilitators also encounter situations in which group members may want to exercise more power than management is comfortable with. In these situations you can help members prepare to negotiate the increased power they want by taking them through a discussion about the power they need and the inherent risks.

Groups need to think through how they will handle increased power.

Center the discussion around the following questions:

- What power and authority do we need? Why?
- What could go wrong if the group had these powers?
- What concerns are management likely to have?
- What checks and balances can be put into place to neutralize potential problems?
- What sorts of communications links and reporting mechanisms should be put into place to make others more comfortable?
- What accountabilities are we prepared to assume individually and as a group?

Once the group is clear about its main negotiation points, representatives from the team need to meet with the appropriate manager. During negotiations, the manager needs to be asked about his or her concerns and which sorts of risks the organization is prepared to tolerate in the interest of trying new ideas.

Whether a group is reluctant to accept additional empowerment or is trying to negotiate for more, it's a key facilitator role to ensure that all group members are clear as to their exact authority levels.

✎ *Notes*

_____

_____

_____

_____

_____

_____

_____

_____

_____

_____

_____

Chapter 4
Creating Participation

I magine yourself at the start of a day-long session with a group of people you barely know and nothing is working. No one is answering questions. Some people look bored. Others seem openly uncomfortable. Everyone looks nervously at the leader whenever you ask a serious question. You start to wonder how you're going to get through the rest of the session!

As a facilitator you shouldn't expect that all your groups will be enthusiastic and engaged. In fact, most groups need considerable warming up and the use of several participation techniques before they'll perform effectively.

Your first step in getting people to participate actively is to understand why they're exhibiting non-participatory behavior. Consider these main barriers to participation:

_____ members may be confused about the topic being discussed

_____ there may be a lack of commitment to the topic under discussion

_____ they may feel unsure about the quality of their personal contributions

_____ they may be insecure about speaking in front of others

_____ they might be afraid of the reactions of their peers

_____ talkative members may "shut down" quieter people

_____ some people may be reluctant to speak up in front of those they consider to be their "superiors"

_____ there may be a low level of trust and openness in the group

_____ some traumatic event may have occurred recently that has left some members feeling withdrawn

_____ the organization may have a history of not listening to or supporting employee suggestions

When planning any session, it's important to assess how participative the members are likely to be. You can do this before the workshop begins by finding out:

_____ whether or not the participants are used to meeting and discussing ideas

_____ how the members feel about speaking up in front of their leader and each other

_____ whether relations between participants are good or strained

_____ if there has been a recent layoff, personal tragedy or other event that might distract participants

_____ if members have well-developed group skills such as listening, debating, decision making, etc.

_____ how the group has managed past meetings

_____ whether the leader or the organization is likely to support the ideas of the group

Always anticipate the potential blocks to active participation and come armed with strategies to overcome them.

69

Creating the Conditions for Full Participation

As a facilitator you need to understand the basic prerequisites for full participation. In general people will participate fully if they:

_____ feel relaxed with the other participants

_____ understand the topic under discussion

_____ have had some say in the planning process

_____ feel committed to the topic

_____ have the information and knowledge needed for fruitful discussion

_____ feel "safe" in expressing their opinions

_____ aren't interfered with or otherwise unduly influenced

_____ trust and have confidence in the facilitator

_____ are comfortable and at ease in the meeting room

_____ feel that the organization will support their ideas

A good rule is that the more resistant a group is likely to be, the more necessary it is to hold interviews or focus groups with members beforehand to get them involved and let them voice their concerns.

Removing the Blocks to Participation

Ensuring that people participate actively is one of your primary responsibilities. There is no excuse for running a meeting that a few people dominate or in which half the group sits in silent withdrawal. Here are some activities you can use to encourage active involvement.

Break the Ice

Even in a group in which members know one another, they need to engage in ice breakers to set a warm and supportive tone. With groups of strangers, ice breakers are even more important. They help people get to know each other and help to remove barriers to speaking in front of strangers.

Books on ice breakers abound. Do your homework so that you have at least four to six simple warm-up exercises handy at all times.

Clarify the Topic

During the planning phase take pains to ensure that each topic to be discussed is clearly defined. For example, if the meeting is being called to solve a problem, ensure that there's a clear problem statement. Regardless of the type of session, a clear statement that describes the purpose of the meeting is a must.

You'll also achieve topic clarity by having a well-defined goal for each discussion. That means getting the group to agree on what they hope to achieve before they start. This aligns the participants toward a common target.

At the start of any session, make sure everyone is clear about the purpose of the meeting by:

It's your job as facilitator to ensure that everyone is heard.

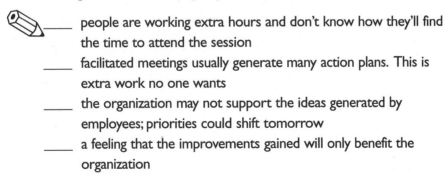

_____ reviewing what created the need for the meeting so that everyone understands its history

_____ sharing the input members gave during any surveys, focus groups or interviews to demonstrate member participation in creating the agenda

_____ asking all present to ratify the purpose statement to ensure full understanding and commitment

_____ stating the goal of the facilitation so everyone is clear about the desired outcome

Always be alert to the fact that even a crystal clear purpose can quickly become cloudy. Members can get sidetracked or suddenly decide there's a more important issue to be discussed. Performing effectively in your role means checking often to make sure that members remain clear about the goal and haven't become confused. This may lead to the realization that the group has indeed been "marching down the wrong road" and now needs to redefine the goal and potentially start over in a new direction.

It's quite common for facilitators to have to redefine the design of a session in midstream. (That's what makes facilitating such a challenge.) The wise facilitator is always open to making changes. Forcing a group to continue a discussion that no longer makes sense, just "because it's on the agenda," is a sure formula for disaster.

Create Buy-In

People are very cynical these days. They feel vulnerable and abused. They work longer hours for less pay. Speculation about layoffs is rampant. Employee morale is generally at an all-time low, and distrust of management is high.

Facilitators who naively think that people are automatically going to be keen and enthusiastic about coming to their session are in for a shock. These days it's especially important to check with your group to determine how many of the following harsh realities are going to be a factor:

_____ people are working extra hours and don't know how they'll find the time to attend the session

_____ facilitated meetings usually generate many action plans. This is extra work no one wants

_____ the organization may not support the ideas generated by employees; priorities could shift tomorrow

_____ a feeling that the improvements gained will only benefit the organization

In today's work environment, you'd be foolish to attempt to run any meeting without gaining commitment and buy-in from the participants.

Getting people to commit is achieved by asking them to answer the universal buy-in question "What's in it for me?"

Always keep your eye on the goal, and make sure it stays clear.

An effective buy-in activity is to pair up participants at the start of any session and ask them to spend five minutes discussing two questions:

"What's the gain for the organization in solving this problem, fixing this process, etc.?"

"How will I personally benefit if we solve this problem, fix this process, etc.?"

After the partner discussion, participants can recount their own or their partner's responses. Record all comments on the flip charts. The participants' responses to the second question amounts to their psychological buy-in to the session. This seems deceptively simple, but is actually a powerful step. Leaving it out can stop people from participating fully.

If participants say there are few benefits but lots of reasons for them not to participate, you'll need to spend more time on the buy-in activity.

In these cases of heightened levels of resistance, add two additional questions to the partner buy-in exercise:

"What's blocking me personally from participating? Why might I be reluctant?"

"What will it take to overcome these blocks? Under what conditions, and with what support, will I consider giving this my full attention?"

When you record members' responses to these two further questions, you'll, in effect, be negotiating their participation. People may say they'll participate if there are assurances from senior management for support of their ideas or that they need to be given time off, help or other compensation for their added efforts. Or they might ask for assurances that the decisions made will be honored. Having their conditions on the table lets you assess the extent to which the participants are feeling blocked.

The problem with identifying the blocks is, of course, that you may not be in a position to negotiate many of these items. If you anticipate strong resistance, it's best to surface the blocks in the planning phase. This allows time to negotiate the support issues before the session. The results of the resistance negotiations can then be presented at the beginning of the session to help relieve concerns and help people move forward with commitment. In high-resistance situations, the manager and even a senior manager may have to be present at the start of the meeting to respond to the conditions set out by the members.

Remember to vary the buy-in question for different situations. To create "buy-in" for a process-improvement exercise, ask group members:

"How will my work life be made easier if we manage to simplify this process?"

To create "buy-in" for joining a team, ask group members:

"What are the possible benefits for me personally, if I become a member of this team?"

Build in the buy-in process at the start of major meetings.

To create "buy-in" for learning a new skill, ask group members:

> *"How is learning to operate the new software going to benefit me in my career?"*

Make Eye Contact

This is a simple but a very important technique to improve participation. You need to make eye contact with *everyone*, not just the active participants. By looking directly at the more quiet people, you're telling them that they haven't been forgotten. Sometimes your glance will actually prompt them to speak up. The eye contact must, of course, be friendly and encouraging, not piercing and intimidating.

Use Humor

Everybody enjoys a good laugh, especially these days. Humor is a great way to create an open atmosphere. How to introduce humor into your session? Have people reveal an amusing anecdote about themselves, show cartoons, or stop periodically for a team game. Running jokes and amusing comments are all useful as long as they're in proper proportion and don't detract from the focus of the session.

Manage the Participation of Leaders

If you're acting as an external facilitator, you'll often be asked to plan and manage meetings in which the group's leader is present. This leader may be the person who contacted you for assistance and who considers him- or herself to be your client.

Leaders are often used to chairing meetings and strongly influencing their outcome. It isn't unheard of for a leader to ask a facilitator to lead a discussion in the direction of a predetermined outcome he or she favors. The harsh reality is that some people see facilitation as a sophisticated tool for manipulating others.

To avoid misunderstanding, the facilitator and leader need to discuss a number of key points. The leader needs to be told tactfully that:

- the leader isn't the client; a facilitator's client is always the whole group, including the leader
- facilitation is a "democratic" undertaking in which the leader must agree to abide by the decisions made by the whole group
- the facilitator reserves the right to personally and privately contact the participants before the session, via interviews or surveys, to gain their input

If the pre-session interviews with staff reveal that the leader is very opinionated and/or that staff are reluctant to speak in the leader's presence, it's within your rights to ask the leader to hold back, so that others can feel free to speak. Every experienced facilitator you'll meet can tell you stories of situations in which he or she had to pull the group leader aside at a break and tell that person to temper his or her participation.

There are also numerous workshop designs in which the leader attends a "kick-off" session, pledges support and then leaves, while the staff work. At the end of

Use eye contact to include quiet people.

If a leader wants to manipulate the session outcome, it's appropriate for the facilitator to decline the assignment.

*Domineering
leaders will
need to be
coached ahead
of time not to
dominate.*

the session the leader returns to hear final recommendations, give any needed approvals and offer to act as an ongoing sponsor of member activities.

If you're lucky enough to have a group whose leader is open and regarded as a valuable colleague by the rest of the members, encourage him or her to play an active role in the entire discussion. After all, one of the reasons leaders bring in facilitators is to free themselves to participate and offer their expertise to the group.

Regardless of the situation, the best strategy is to explain the parameters of your role as facilitator clearly at the beginning of the session.

Help Participants Prepare

We all know what a colossal waste of time a meeting can be if no one is prepared and people are forced to make decisions without adequate information. To prevent this from happening at your session, make sure the purpose of the meeting is clear and communicate this information before the meeting so that people have time to get ready. If the meeting is expected to be complex, have a small group meet ahead of time to identify who needs to do which portion of the "homework." If the group is small, you might call all people to make sure they understand their "homework" assignments.

When people do adequate pre-work, they gain confidence and will often participate much more actively.

Create Targeted Norms

All groups need guidelines to ensure a cooperative and supportive climate. As mentioned earlier in this book, rules should be written by the participants themselves, in response to the question, "What rules should we agree to govern ourselves by throughout this meeting?" An example of common meeting norms can be found on page 55.

If there seems to be a significant amount of reluctance to speak up, the group can create specific, targeted norms to ensure that members feel safe enough to participate. "Safety" norms are an example of targeted norms. In this case, norms are created for the comfort of participants who may feel that they're operating in a particularly sensitive environment.

Help members create safety norms by asking the questions:

> *"What rules should we establish today that will ensure that no one feels
> he or she can't speak up with confidence? Under what conditions are
> you going to be able to speak your mind freely?"*

Some sample "safety" norms include:
- all ideas are good and will be listened to carefully
- all discussions are strictly confidential (i.e. "what's said here, stays here")
- both people and issues will be handled with respect
- all ideas will be handled seriously and with sincerity
- there will be no retaliation on the basis of anything that is said in this meeting
- no one will personally attack another person

- all feedback must be phrased in a constructive manner and be aimed at helping the other person
- if anyone feels emotionally stressed, he or she can call "time out" and request a change in how a topic is being handled
- everyone will use neutral body language (i.e. "no pointing, shaking fingers, crossing arms, etc.")
- instead of just arguing our points, we'll listen to and acknowledge each other's ideas first
- anyone can call a time out if he or she is confused about the topic or feels that the discussion is going off track

Targeted norms may also be necessary in a range of other situations.
- If the group has experienced **conflict**, ask a norming question such as:

> *"What rules do we need to set today to ensure we manage conflict at this meeting?"*

- If any members of the group are **reluctant to participate**, ask:

> *"What guidelines should we establish that will encourage participation and help all members feel their ideas are important?"*

- If the group has trouble **staying on track**, ask:

> *"What rules will help ensure that we stay on track and on time today?"*

As with regular norms, targeted norms need to be developed by the participants, in response to specific situations. If there's no response when you ask the norming question, divide members into pairs or subgroups to answer the norming question. Then, gather up their ideas.

Specific situations need targeted norms.

Set Up the Room to Encourage Participation

It's a factor that may not seem obvious at first, but how you arrange a room will greatly affect how group members interact. Theater-style seating is the worst possible arrangement for facilitating an active discussion. People automatically assume that they'll be spoken at. It also discourages people from looking at each other.

Large boardroom tables have an especially stifling effect on people. This is very unfortunate, as many large companies have huge boardroom tables stuck squarely in the middle of their best meeting room. If this room is your only option, break people into pairs, trios and foursomes as often as possible to keep everyone talking.

If you have any choice in the matter of seating, select a large room and try to get small, modular tables. Small rectangles arranged in a large horseshoe for whole group sessions or smaller squares for small group discussions are the best.

If the group has more than ten people, break it into small groups of not more than eight people per group. People can sit in their small groups, even when the whole group is in session. Small groups always help break the ice and create a more private forum for discussions.

Clarify Your Role

Near the beginning of any facilitation, tell participants why you're there and what you'll be doing. Be clear that you'll make sure everyone is heard, that you'll work hard to keep the topic on track and that you'll be remaining neutral on all topics.

Offer your own criteria and hopes for a successful meeting, so people know you intend to contribute to a productive and constructive session. Don't be afraid to brag about yourself a bit. Some participants will be more likely to speak up if they have confidence in your skills.

Identify the Organizational Supports

Recognize past frustrations that members have had with organizational blocks.

If the pre-workshop interviews reveal that people are worried that the session might be an exercise in futility, be sure to express these concerns to the appropriate manager. There is nothing worse than having members balk at the start of a workshop because they're worried that their ideas won't be supported. If organizational barriers can be dealt with before the session, that will help create a much more positive environment.

Another common strategy is to have a senior manager attend the kick-off portion of the meeting to offer his or her personal assurance of support for the group's efforts. If this isn't possible, a memo or letter from the senior manager expressing strong support is a help.

If there's no senior management support, and the barriers are a major concern, it's important to surface these issues and discuss them, rather than pretend they don't exist. Set aside time at the end of the workshop to identify the barriers, analyze them and generate solutions for getting around them. This way members will feel that the discussions have been honest and that they have strategies for dealing with the realities they face.

High-Participation Techniques

There are many excellent techniques available to get even the most reluctant and shy participant to play an active part. These techniques offer anonymity to members and generate lots of activity.

1. Discussion Partners

This simple technique can be used as a way of starting any discussion. After posing a question to a large group, ask everyone to find a partner and discuss the question for a few minutes. Have people report on what they talked about. You can use this with threesomes as well.

2. Tossed Salad

Place an empty cardboard box or an inexpensive plastic salad bowl on the table. Give out small slips of paper and ask people to write down one good idea per slip. Have them toss the slips into the bowl. When people have finished writing, have someone "toss the salad." Pass around the bowl so that each person can take out as many slips as they tossed in. Go around the table and have people share ideas before discussing and refining the most promising ones together.

3. Issues and Answers

When faced with a long list of issues to tackle, rather than attempting to problem-solve all of them as a whole group (which would take forever), post the problems around the room. Put only one issue on each sheet of flip chart paper.

Ask all members to go to one of the issue sheets and discuss that problem with whomever else was drawn to that sheet. Make sure people are distributed evenly, with at least three people per issue. You can use chairs, but this works best as a stand-up activity.

Allow up to five minutes for the subgroups to analyze the situation. Have them make notes on the top half of the flip chart sheet. Ring a bell and ask everyone to move to another flip chart sheet. When they get there, ask them to read the analysis made by the first group and to add any additional ideas. This round is often shorter than five minutes. Keep moving people around until everyone is back at his or her original sheet.

Once the analysis round is complete, ask everyone to return to the original issue he or she started with. Ask them to generate and record solutions to their respective issue on the bottom half of the sheet. Once again circulate people until everyone has added ideas on all of the sheets.

To end the process have everyone walk by each sheet, read the solutions and check off the one or two ideas they think are the best.

When everyone is seated again, go through the ideas together and then ask the small groups to each take responsibility for creating action plans for the ideas on one of the sheets.

4. Talk Circuit

This technique works best in a large crowd because it creates a strong buzz and lets people get to know each other. Start by posing a question to the group and then allow quiet time for each person to write his or her own response.

Ask everyone to sit "knee to knee" with a partner and share their ideas. Have one person speak while the other acts as facilitator. After two to three minutes ring a bell and have partners reverse their roles. After two or three more minutes stop the discussions.

Ask everyone to find a new partner and repeat the process, but in slightly less time. Stop the action and then have everyone repeat the process with a third partner.

In the final round allow only one minute per person. When the partner discussions are over, discuss the ideas as a whole group and record them on flip charts.

5. Pass the Envelope

Give each person an envelope filled with blank slips of paper. Pose a question or challenge to the group, and then have everyone write down as many ideas as they can within the given time frame and put the slips into the envelope. Tell people to pass the envelopes, either to the next person or in all directions, and when the passing stops, read the contents. Pair off participants and have them discuss the ideas in their envelope. What ideas did they receive? What are the positives and negatives of each idea? What other ideas should they add? Combine pairs to form groups of four and ask them to further refine the content of their four envelopes into practical action plans. Hold a plenary to collect ideas.

Break up large groups and use a variety of techniques to maintain participation.

Use this survey if there's concern that all members aren't participating fully. For the steps in conducting and feeding back the results see page 166 or 193.

 Group Effectiveness Survey

Instructions to Members:

Read over the following statements and rate how your group currently manages the participation of its members. Be totally honest. Remember that this survey is anonymous. The results will be tabulated and fed back to the group for their assessment.

1. **Commitment** — Member commitment to our goal is high

1	2	3	4	5
totally disagree	disagree somewhat	not sure	agree somewhat	totally agree

2. **Acceptance** — Members are friendly, concerned and interested in each other

1	2	3	4	5
totally disagree	disagree somewhat	not sure	agree somewhat	totally agree

3. **Belonging** — Members feel a close bond with each other

1	2	3	4	5
totally disagree	disagree somewhat	not sure	agree somewhat	totally agree

4. **Involvement** — All members play an active role. The group isn't dominated by one or two strong individuals

1	2	3	4	5
totally disagree	disagree somewhat	not sure	agree somewhat	totally agree

5. **Support** — Members listen to and respect each other's views

1	2	3	4	5
totally disagree	disagree somewhat	not sure	agree somewhat	totally agree

6. **Respect** — Members appreciate each other's different strengths. Everyone is valued for his or her specific skills

1	2	3	4	5
totally disagree	disagree somewhat	not sure	agree somewhat	totally agree

7. **Tolerance** — Members recognize and accept individual differences

1	2	3	4	5
totally disagree	disagree somewhat	not sure	agree somewhat	totally agree

8. **Recognition** — Members give each other positive feedback about excellent performance

1	2	3	4	5
totally disagree	disagree somewhat	not sure	agree somewhat	totally agree

Encouraging Effective Meeting Behaviors

Sometimes you'll find yourself working with groups whose members behave as though they were being paid bonuses for rudeness. People interrupt. Members run in and out. People dismiss ideas before they've really tried to understand them, and so on.

Producing outcomes is a battle in these situations. The wisest thing to do is stop the proceedings and give the members a crash course in effective meeting behaviors.

This mini-training session is simple, quick and surprisingly effective. It consists of the following steps:

1. Introduce the idea that certain behaviors are less effective than others. Hand out the sheets on the next two pages, which describe effective and ineffective meeting behaviors. Go over each behavior described. Answer any questions.

2. Appoint one member of the group to be the observer for the rest of the meeting. Give this person the observation sheet and ask him or her to make note of all occurrences of the listed behaviors. This means keeping track of both the names of people and the specific thing done or said. (This observer may need to sit on the sidelines during the discussion, although some people are able to observe and also participate.)

3. At the end of the session, set aside some time to hear from the observer. Were there more effective or ineffective behaviors displayed? What were some specific examples of each type?

4. Ask members for their observations. At the end of this discussion, the group should be asked to write new norms by which to govern itself.

Never continue facilitating a session in which people behave dysfunctionally!

Group Behaviors Handout

In order to be effective when working together, we all need to be aware of individual and collective behaviors.

Behaviors That Help Effectiveness:

Behavior	Description
Listens Actively	looks at the person who is speaking, nods, asks probing questions and acknowledges what is said by paraphrasing point(s) made
Supports	encourages others to develop ideas and make suggestions; gives them recognition for their ideas
Probes	goes beyond the surface comments by questioning teammates to uncover hidden information
Clarifies	asks members for more information about what they mean; clears up confusion
Offers Ideas	shares suggestions, ideas, solutions and proposals
Includes Others	asks quiet members for their opinions, making sure no one is left out
Summarizes	pulls together ideas from a number of people; determines where the group is and what has been covered
Harmonizes	reconciles opposing points of view; links together similar ideas; points out where ideas are the same
Manages Conflict	listens to the views of others; clarifies issues and key points made by opponents; seeks solutions

Behaviors That Hinder Effectiveness:

Behavior	Description
"Yeah But's"	discredits the ideas of others
Blocks	insists on getting one's way; doesn't compromise; stands in the way of the team's progress
Grandstands	draws attention to one's personal skills; boasts
Goes Off Topic	directs the conversation off onto other topics
Dominates	tries to "run" the group through dictating, bullying
Withdraws	doesn't participate or offer help or support to others
Devil's Advocate	takes pride in being contrary
Criticizes	makes negative comments about people or their ideas
Personal Slurs	hurls insults at other people

Observing Group Behaviors in Action

Write down any specific examples of the following behaviors. Include the name of the person and some details about what he or she did.

EFFECTIVE	INEFFECTIVE
Actively listens	*Yeah but's*
Supports	*Blocks*
Probes	*Grandstands*
Clarifies	*Goes off topic*
Offers ideas	*Dominates*
Includes others	*Withdraws*
Summarizes	*Devil's advocate*
Harmonizes	*Criticizes*
Manages conflict	*Personal slurs*

Peer Review

There are times when group members need to receive feedback from each other. This may be necessary when they're experiencing conflict or when individuals are letting down the team.

The peer feedback format consists of two areas of focus, both of which have a positive intent. The first lets people praise each other. The second offers supportive advice to help the other person improve. These areas are:

1. What you do that's really effective. (Keep on doing it!)

2. What you could do that would make you even more effective.

Here's how everyone can participate in this powerful feedback exercise:

Step 1: Each member writes his or her name at the top of a blank Peer Review Format worksheet on the next page and then passes it to the right.

Step 2: Each member answers both questions about the person whose name is at the top of each sheet.

Step 3: Sheets are passed around the table until everyone has written comments about each member.

Step 4: Each person eventually gets back the sheet with his or her own name on it, completely filled out with comments from all of the other members.

Step 5: The process can stop here, with each person keeping his or her own feedback, or you can ask people to:
- pass the completed sheets around again, and have people read aloud the positive comments they wrote about the other person. This is called a "strength bombardment."
- Have members choose partners to discuss what they learned from their feedback and create action plans for personal change. End with members sharing their action steps with the group.

This form of peer review is non-threatening, because no one receives negative comments, as both feedback questions are positive and forward-looking.

This exercise is extremely effective because the coaching advice is coming from peers. It subtly reminds members of the importance of meeting each other's needs and expectations. If tensions develop between people, this feedback method allows them to safely request what they need from each other. Since peer feedback often resolves interpersonal conflicts before they flare up, it's a good activity to do periodically as a preventative measure.

Harness the power of peer feedback to manage member behaviors.

Peer Review Format

Name: _____ **Date:** _____

(of person receiving the feedback)

_____

What you do that's really effective. (Keep on doing it!)

_____

What you could do that would make you even more effective.

✎ *Notes*

Chapter 5
Facilitating Conflict

Dealing with conflict is a fact of every facilitator's life. Accepting that conflict is inevitable, and being prepared to deal with it, will only work to your advantage!

Consider the following scenario: Imagine yourself facilitating an important meeting. Everything is going along great until you hit agenda item #3. Suddenly two members start arguing. Listening goes out the window, as each person pushes his or her ideas. The rest of the group gets uncomfortable, as the two combatants become more and more emotional. The discussion spins in circles and people get upset!

What do you do now? For starters, rather than seeing conflict as a disaster, you need to view conflict as a positive sign that people care about the issue and have energy to put toward solutions. What determines whether conflict deteriorates into a disaster or leads to a challenging debate is how it's handled.

Knowing the Difference Between Debates and Arguments

All facilitators need to be attuned to the differences between a debate and an argument. Healthy debate is essential. If a group doesn't express differences of opinion, then it's basically incapable of making effective decisions. Dysfunctional arguments, on the other hand, lead to disaster!

Differences of opinion are not only inevitable but vital for making good decisions.

In Healthy Debates	In Dysfunctional Arguments
→ people are open to hearing other's ideas	→ people assume they're right
→ people listen and respond to ideas even if they don't agree with them	→ people wait until others have finished talking, then state their ideas without responding to ideas of the other person
→ everyone tries to understand the views of the other person	→ no one is interested in how the other person sees the situation
→ people stay objective and focus on the facts	→ people get personally attacked and blamed
→ there's a systematic approach to analyzing the situation and looking for solutions	→ hot topics get thrashed out in an unstructured way

It's your approach that will determine whether people debate or argue.

Techniques that Create Healthy Debate	Techniques that Allow Dysfunctional Arguments
➜ stay totally neutral	➜ join the argument
➜ point out differences so they can be understood	➜ ignore differences – just pray they will go away
➜ insist that people listen politely – have rules and use them	➜ let people be rude – set no norms
➜ make people paraphrase each other's ideas	➜ ignore the fact that no one is really hearing anyone else
➜ ask for concerns	➜ sidestep hot issues
➜ make people focus on facts	➜ let people get personal
➜ problem solve concerns	➜ get defensive
➜ invite and face feedback	➜ squash dissent
➜ facilitate assertively	➜ stand by passively
➜ get closure and move on	➜ let it drag on and on

Steps in Managing Conflict—Overview

Facilitating conflict has two distinct steps:

Step 1: Venting

This involves listening to people so that they feel heard and so that any built-up emotions are diffused. People are rarely ready to move on to solutions until their emotional blocks have been removed.

Step 2: Resolving the issue

Choosing the right structured approach to get to solutions. This can be a collaborative problem-solving activity, compromising, accommodating or consciously avoiding.

Let's look at each step in more detail.

Step 1: Venting People's Emotions

Not every difference of opinion is characterized by intense emotions. There are groups who objectively surface issues, calmly discuss the facts, listen politely to each other and collaborate to find the best solution.

Unfortunately you won't encounter them often enough. More often, facilitators see any of the following behaviors in conflict situations:

- people pushing their points of view, without being at all receptive to the ideas of others
- people becoming angry, defensive and personal with each other
- negative body language, like glaring and finger pointing
- sarcastic or dismissive remarks
- people "yeah butting" and criticizing each other's ideas
- quiet people "shutting down" to stay out of it
- extreme anger to the point where relationships are damaged

People won't move forward to resolve a problem until their feelings have been dealt with.

It is the facilitator's job to properly handle negative emotions as soon as they emerge, so that they don't poison the dynamics of the group. When people start to get emotional there are some basic strategies that the facilitator should employ:

- **Slow things down** – get the attention of the group by stopping the action and asking people to slow down. You can use the excuse that you can't take notes as quickly as people are talking. Ask them to start over and repeat key ideas.

- **Stay totally neutral** – never take sides or allow your body language to hint that you favor one idea or one person over another.

- **Stay calm** – maintain your composure and do not raise your own voice. Speak slowly with an even tone. Avoid emotional body language.

- **Revisit the norms** – point out the existing norms and remind people that they agreed to them earlier on. Engage the group in writing new norms.

- **Be assertive** – move into the referee mode. Insist that people speak one at a time. Make them put their hands up and stop people who interrupt others. Don't stand by passively while people fight.

- **Raise awareness** – on a clean sheet of flip chart paper record member ideas about the difference between a debate versus an argument. Ask them which one they want to have.

- **Make interventions** – don't let people fight with each other or display rudeness. Refer to pages 95 in this chapter for the appropriate wording for different interventions.

- **Emphasize listening** – paraphrase key points and ask others to do the same thing. Hand out, discuss, and then enforce the practices outlined on page 88.

- **Call time out** – don't hesitate to stop the action any time emotions get out of hand or if the discussion is spinning in circles. Ask: *"Are we making progress? Are we using the right approach? How are people feeling?"* Act on their suggestions for improving the meeting. Refer to page 43 on process checking for more on how to handle time-outs.

- **Use a structured approach** – use techniques such as force-field analysis, multi-voting, systematic problem solving, cause and effect analysis, etc. Don't let a discussion rage on without imposing structure and systematically capturing key ideas. Chapter 8 provides detailed descriptions of the most commonly used facilitator tools.

- **Use the flip chart** – make note of key points so they aren't lost and the group members don't have to go over the whole thing again. Read back the notes on the flip chart whenever you want to regain control for a few minutes.

- **Create closure** – make sure that the debating is really going somewhere. Ask group members to help summarize what has been agreed to. Test these items for agreement. Help the group create action plans to ensure implementation of key suggestions.

In conflicts you need to facilitate calmly yet assertively!

Listen-Empathize-Clarify-Seek Permission-Resolve

1. Listen – Instead of arguing when you hear a point you disagree with, listen attentively to the person's main points. Let people vent their feelings. Look interested and concerned. Say any of these things:

> *"Tell me more. That's interesting. Uh-huh.*
> *I'm not sure I understand. Could you go over that again?"*

2. Empathize – Accept the views of the other person even if you don't agree with them. Let people know you understand their feelings. Say:

> *"I don't blame you for feeling that way. I see what you mean.*
> *I understand how you feel. I'm sure I'd feel the same way if...."*

3. Clarify – Delve deeper to ensure that you have a clear understanding of what the other person is saying to you. Say:

> *"Let me see if I've got it straight; what you're saying is....*
> *Is it possible that....The idea you're proposing is...."*

4. Seek Permission – Tell your side after the other person has expressed all of his or her concerns and feels clearly understood. Say:

> *"Now that I understand your views, can I explain mine?"*
> *"It seems that this would be a good time to bring up a few points you haven't mentioned."*

5. Resolve the Issue – Once you have both heard each other, this is the time to start dealing with the problem together.

Step 2: Resolving Issues

Here are five basic approaches you can choose from, once emotions have been vented, in order to resolve the underlying issue:

Avoid ignore the conflict in the hope that it will go away. Maintain silence or try to change the subject.

Accommodate ask people to be more tolerant and accept each other's views. Ask them to try getting along. This sometimes involves asking one person to give in to another person.

Compromise look for the middle ground between highly polarized views. Ask each person to give up some of what he or she wants, in order to get other items he or she thinks are more important.

Compete use force to make points and quell any conflicts. Go for a personal win even if the other person feels like he or she has lost the argument.

Collaborate face the conflict, draw people's attention to it, surface the issues and resolve them in a win/win way by using systematic problem solving.

Hand out copies of the L-E-C-S-R sheet if people need reminders about how to act.

The Five Conflict Options: Pros and Cons

Each of the aforementioned approaches can work in specific situations. Facilitators need to understand each one and choose the one that suits the situation.

Avoiding – When conflict is avoided, nothing gets resolved. Yet this is the right approach to use if the issue at stake is very trivial, can't be solved or will result in a total lose/lose situation for the group. Avoiding is sometimes a wise interim strategy to give people a chance to calm down before addressing issues.

The main consequence of avoiding is that issues aren't resolved and there's no creativity applied towards finding a solution. The problem remains to fester and can crop up later. While avoiding has its place, groups become very ineffective if they avoid most of their issues.

Accommodating – This is a social response aimed more at keeping the peace than solving the problem. This approach can involve asking everyone to just get along or asking one party in a conflict to give in to the other party.

Accommodating is the appropriate approach in situations in which one person is only slightly interested in the issue, while the other party cares deeply. It's also the right approach to take when exploration of the issue reveals that one party is wrong. This style is most applicable to family and other social gatherings in which tolerance and civility may be of greater importance than finding the right answer.

The consequence of accommodating is that the underlying issues are often left unexplored in the interest of keeping the peace.

Compromising – This is a mediated approach to managing conflict that is used when two people or two groups have formulated strong positions. Neither party feels he or she can accept the position of the other, so a neutral middle option has to be developed.

The good thing about compromising is that it does yield a solution. The problem is that both parties must give up some favored points to get others. The process of compromise also tends to be adversarial. People argue their sides in the hopes of winning specific items.

At the end of a compromise, people feel that they have both won and lost. They may also harbor some negative feelings towards the other party because the process is largely adversarial. Compromise leaves people feeling, "I'm going to have to live with it!"

Competing – This is a strategy of defending oneself and arguing one's point of view in order to score a win over the another person. Competing is a contest of wills, in which the person who wins does so at the expense of the other person.

Competing has its place in those situations that are clearly defined as competitive, such as sports and war. In these situations, the winner is less apt to worry about the feelings of the loser.

While competing does yield a solution, it's combative and emotional. This approach has no place in the repertoire of the facilitator.

When people are upset, avoiding conflict is sometimes a wise interim strategy.

In some conflict situations, one party ought to be encouraged to think about giving in.

Compromising is adversarial and can leave people divided.

Competing is a totally unacceptable strategy for solving a problem inside a team.

Collaboration promotes a win/win outcome.

Collaboration – This is a "consensus"-building process. It involves identifying the issue and then engaging all members of the group in analyzing it fully, generating creative ideas, objectively sorting through potential solutions and agreeing on a course of action to resolve the issue. This is basically using a systematic problem-solving approach to deal with conflict.

This approach starts by engaging everyone in analyzing the situation, rather than jumping right to solutions. It relies on objective information. Everyone inputs ideas. People are encouraged to listen and build on each other's points. Solutions are generated through the use of non-competitive processes such as brainstorming. The best course of action is determined by applying a set of criteria to the choices available.

At the end of a collaboration, everyone feels that he or she was heard and that the final strategy reflects his or her thinking. While the final outcome may not be exactly what they would have decided on their own, all members feel that they have had a say. Because collaboration emphasizes working together for a win/win, it creates a consensus. At the end of a conflict resolved through collaboration, people's feelings about the solution are: "I can live with it!"

The main drawback to collaboration (consensus) is that it requires a great deal of time and thus may result in a waste of energy if used on an insignificant issue.

The Five Options in Action

Consider the following conflict situation:

Fred and Bill are getting very heated talking about whether or not to conduct classroom computer training for the new software about to be introduced in the department.

Fred thinks that hands-on help, while people work with the system, is the way to go. He thinks the proposed two days of classroom time is costly and takes people off the job for too long.

Bill is arguing that the new system is too complex for people to learn on the job and that too many mistakes will be made if people learn through trial and error.

Now consider possible facilitator responses using each of the five conflict options. Which work? Which don't? Why?

The facilitator fosters avoidance

> *"You two seem quite deadlocked. Let's move on and discuss something else within our remaining time."*

The facilitator encourages accommodation

> *"Look Bill, Fred is pretty adamant that his people not be off the job for any length of time. Since most of the staff are in his department, could you forget the idea of training classes?"*

The facilitator competes

> *"Fred, don't you think hands-on training is a bit hit-and-miss?"*

The facilitator suggests a compromise

> *"Is there a middle ground such as giving people a shorter classroom session and still supporting them with hands-on training?"*

The facilitator uses a collaborative technique

"Let's put all of the facts of the situation on the table. What are the details of our work and time pressures? Which skills do people need? What are all the possible options for getting people trained? What are the characteristics of the best options? Which of our options looks like it meets those criteria? What are we going to do?

In the above five scenarios you will have noticed:

Avoiding doesn't deal with the issue	↪ Use it in those 10% of situations when issues can't be resolved profitably
Accommodating just smoothes things over	↪ Use it only in those 5% of situations when keeping the peace is of more importance than finding a solution
Competing divides groups and creates win/lose	↪ Facilitators should never compete! Zero percent applicability
Compromise seeks to find the middle ground	↪ Use it in those 20% of situations when faced with polarized choices
Collaboration gets people working together to find the best solution for everyone	↪ This as the #1 preferred approach for all facilitators. Use it in 65% of all conflict situations

Collaboration encourages people to work together to objectively seek solutions that they can all live with. Because it's consensual, it unites and generates solutions that everyone feels committed to implementing. It's the superior conflict option!

Assumptions underlying collaboration:

Collaboration is a superior way of solving a problem during a meeting; however, a number of conditions need to be in place to ensure a successful outcome. Members must:

__ have sufficient trust among themselves to open up and be supportive of each other when necessary

__ have a positive intent to work towards a win/win solution

__ have relevant information on hand to make a sound decision

__ have the time to make this decision

__ believe the topic is important enough to warrant spending the time it will take

Collaboration is the preferred style for facilitating all disputes within any group or team.

Conflict Management Norms

Anytime you anticipate that a session has the potential to become contentious or if the group has had stormy meetings in the past, it's a good idea to create specially targeted norms for conflict situations. As with all other norms, these are created by the members, preferably at the start of the session. Use the following questions to trigger the discussion:

> *"What behaviors and rules should we adhere to if we find ourselves getting into serious disagreements?*
> *What can we do to ensure that we have a good debate instead of a heated argument?"*

Some sample norms targeted at conflict situations include:

- we'll speak one at a time
- we'll look at each other when we speak and acknowledge any valid points made by the other person
- we'll accept all ideas as valid when presented
- we'll build on each other's ideas
- we won't dismiss any idea without really exploring it
- we'll make sure everyone is heard – not just a few people
- we won't get emotional, argumentative or personal
- no one will attack anyone else
- if the discussion gets heated or we start going in circles, we'll call a time-out and look at how we are doing things
- no one will deliberately block the group from reaching a final solution by taking a position
- we'll take a systematic approach to resolving issues rather than just pushing personal points of view

Once conflict norms are established, they should be referred to at strategic moments, to make sure they're being followed. Sometimes adding a new norm in the middle of a conflict discussion helps to stabilize the situation.

Norms are your best tool for heading off potential conflict.

Making Interventions

During any workshop or meeting, there are many occasions when the facilitator will need to make an intervention. The definition of "intervention" is, "any action or set of actions deliberately taken to improve the functioning of the group." This may be necessary in situations in which:

- someone isn't listening
- two people are having a side conversation
- people are interrupting each other
- one person uses a sarcastic tone during a debate
- people's comments get personal
- the discussion is getting off track

Intervening is like holding up a mirror to the participants so that they can see what they're doing and take steps to correct the problem.

Regardless of its length and complexity, an intervention is always an interruption. You stop the group's discussion about the task and draw members' attention to an aspect of the process. Since this constitutes an interruption in the flow of discussion, the aim is always to resolve the problem as quickly as possible so that the members can return to their task.

The need to intervene may arise because of one individual, or it may be interpersonal, involving a conflict between two or more people.

Groups can also experience problems that involve all of the members, such as poor listening, or a problem that stems from using the wrong process, for example, using a force-field analysis instead of cause and effect analysis.

You always need to be cautious about whether or not to intervene. If you intervened every single time there was a problem, you might be interrupting too frequently. Instead, you need to keep a watchful eye for repetitive, inappropriate behaviors that don't seem to resolve themselves.

When members act inappropriately, facilitators need to make interventions to redirect people's actions.

Deciding Whether or Not to Intervene

Below is a set of questions to ask when deciding if an intervention is advisable.

___ Is the problem serious?
___ Might it go away by itself?
___ How much time will intervening take? Do we have that time?
___ How much of a disruption will intervening cause?
___ How will it impact relationships, the flow of the meeting?
___ Can the intervention hurt the climate?
___ Will it damage anyone's self-esteem?
___ What's the chance that the intervention will work or fail?
___ Do I know these people well enough to do this?
___ Do I have enough credibility to do this?
___ Is it appropriate given their level of openness and trust?

Finally, a good question to ask yourself is, "What will happen if I do nothing?" If the answer is that the group will be less effective if you do nothing, you're obligated to take action.

Failing to make an intervention, when one is truly needed, constitutes weak facilitation.

Wording Interventions

Interventions are always risky because they can make the situation worse. For this reason, interventions need to be worded carefully. There are generally three distinct components to an intervention statement:

Step 1:   **Describe** what you're seeing – this is non-judgmental and doesn't attribute motive. It's based solely on observations of actual events, i.e. *"Allen and Sue, both of you have left and returned three times during this meeting."*

Step 2: *Make an impact statement.* Tell members how their actions
are impacting on you, the process, or other people. Base this on
actual observations, i.e. *"We had to stop our discussions and start
over again on three occasions because of your comings and goings over
the last hour."*

Step 2: *Make an impact statement.* Tell members how their actions
are impacting on you, the process, or other people. Base this on
actual observations, i.e. *"We had to stop our discussions and start
over again on three occasions because of your comings and goings over
the last hour."*

Step 3: *Redirect* the person's behavior(s) – this can be done by:
(a) asking members for their suggestions about what to do,
i.e. *"What can you do to make sure this doesn't happen again?"*
(b) telling members what to do, i.e. *"Please either leave or stay for
the rest of the meeting."*

<u>**Special Note:**</u> *Impact statements (Step 2 above) can be omitted from an interven-
tions if they are interpreted as laying excessive guilt on the offending parties. You need
to use your judgment as to whether or not the situation requires a focus on "impact." A
good rule of thumb is to use impact statements when the offensive behavior is persistent
or repetitive and previous intervention attempts have been ignored.*

Common Intervention Language

Since the wording of interventions is so important, here are some sentence
stems that are commonly used:

"I'm noticing that..."

"I'd like to offer this observation...."

"Let's stop for a moment and look at what's happening here."

"It strikes me that..."

"What are people experiencing right now?"

"I'd like to suggest the following...."

"How do people feel that things have gone thus far?"

"A pattern I have observed is...."

"I'd like to describe what I am seeing here and get your reaction to it."

"You seem to be...."

Intervention Wording for Specific Situations

If group members begin exhibiting behaviors that interfere with progress or
cause stress, there are specific responses you can use. You will notice that none
of these redirecting statements puts down the person or is in any way critical.
All of them offer the other person a chance to save face and to say or do the
right thing next time.

*Interventions
have to be
worded
carefully.*

When someone is being <u>sarcastic</u>:

> *"Ellen, I'm afraid your good ideas aren't being heard because of the tone of voice you're using. How about stating that again, only in a more neutral way?"*

When one person is <u>putting down</u> the ideas of another:

> *"Joe, you have been 'yes butting' every suggestion Carol has put on the table. I'm going to ask you to explore these ideas by asking a few questions to make sure you fully understand them before dismissing them. It will make Carol feel more like she's being heard."*

When two people are <u>arguing</u>, cutting each other off and not listening to each other:

> *"I'm afraid neither of you is hearing the excellent points being made by the other. I'm going to ask you both to first paraphrase what the other has said before you make your own comment."*

When someone is inappropriately <u>aggressive</u> or hurtful to another person:

> *"Fred, I'm going to stop you from saying anything further for just a moment and ask June to tell you how she would like to have you interact with her during the rest of this meeting. June, what would be better than this?"*

When one person <u>dominates</u> the discussion:

> *"Al, you always have lots of valuable ideas, but we need to hear from the other members of the team. Would you please hold your comments until the end so that other people can be heard."*

When someone has hurled a <u>personal slur</u> at someone else:

> *"Jim, rather than characterizing Sally as being 'sloppy,' please tell her specifically about the state of the meeting room after her session, so that she can address the situation."*

When two people are <u>trashing</u> each other's ideas without giving them a fair hearing:

> *"You are discounting each other's ideas very quickly. I'm going to ask that you give a quick recap of what the other person said before launching into your points."*

When a person makes only <u>negative remarks</u> about the ideas of another person:

> *"Mary, what do you like about what Chuck just said?"*

When people <u>run in and out</u> of a meeting:

> *"In the last ten minutes, three people have gone in and out of this meeting, disrupting the discussion. What ought to be done about this?"*

When everyone has <u>fallen silent:</u>

"Everyone has become pretty quiet in the last few minutes and we haven't had any new ideas. What can we do to get things going again?"

When the whole group is acting <u>dysfunctional:</u>

"I'm going to stop this discussion. I'm noticing that two people are talking among themselves while three others are arguing emotionally. What can we do to make the rest of this meeting run more smoothly?"

Members are <u>disregarding</u> their previously set <u>norms:</u>

"I'm going to suggest we stop this meeting for a few minutes to look back at the norms we set last week. Are we following them? Do we need to add a few new ones?"

When the meeting has <u>totally digressed:</u>

"I need to point out that we have now digressed and are onto another topic. Is this the topic the team wants to discuss or should we park it and go back to the original agenda item?"

Telling Versus Asking

In some of the preceding interventions, the facilitator told people what to do, while in others they were asked. Still in others, it sounded like the facilitator was only making a suggestion.

When you're making an intervention you need to make a judgment about which of these approaches to use, situation by situation. While there are no hard and fast rules, here are some principles:

- asking is always better than telling because people are more likely to accept their own intervention
- it's always appropriate for facilitators to suggest or tell people what to do on matters of process
- a directive or telling response is appropriate if the individuals are exhibiting extremely dysfunctional behavior
- the more a group acts maturely and responsibly, the more effective it is to ask, rather than tell

> *The best interventions are the ones that the facilitator gets the group to make themselves!*

Dealing with Resistance

As a facilitator you always need to have a strategy ready for dealing with situations in which a group resists. Groups can resist your facilitation efforts for a number of reasons:

- the timing or location of the meeting might be poor
- the topic of the meeting may not reflect their needs
- they may have received insufficient notice of the meeting
- they're afraid of taking on a new task that entails taking risks
- they suspect that nothing will happen as a result of the meeting
- they feel that the organization isn't behind them, etc.

> *Facilitators should accept that resistance might take place.*

Sometimes this resistance comes out into the open when an outspoken member gets up and vents concern. At other times it remains hidden, only expressed in people's negative body language or lack of participation.

When you encounter resistance, there's a right and a wrong way to deal with it. Using the wrong way will make the resistance grow. Choosing the right approach will make it manageable.

Resistance Scenarios Exercise

To help you become attuned to dealing with resistance, read the following scenarios and see whether you can figure out what makes one response better than the other:

Resistance Scenario #1

Someone says:

> *"The last time we had a two-day retreat nothing happened afterwards. All the promises made were forgotten. People's projects went unsupported. These things are a waste of time!"*

Wrong thing to say:

> *"Well, we're here now and you've each been handpicked to do this project. Senior management is expecting you to do this. You have to accept that organizations are tough places to get things done. This is no time to turn back."*

Right approach for handling resistance:

> *A. "Explain why you feel that way? What happened in the past? How did it impact you?"*
>
> *B. "What would make you a willing participant this time? Under what circumstances or with what assurances will you consider taking up this challenge?"*

Resistance Scenario #2

Someone says:

> *"This meeting is a waste of time. We all have tons of work to do back at the office. I suggest we adjourn right now!"*

Wrong thing to say:

> *"We're here now and some good progress has already been made. We booked the room. It will take months for all of us to coordinate our schedules again. We've even ordered lunch!"*

Right approach for handling resistance:

> *A. "I want to hear why you think this meeting is a waste of time. What has gone on so far today that has caused this frustration?"*
>
> *B. "What changes can we make to the day to eliminate your main concerns? Under which circumstances would you consider staying?"*

Resistance Scenario #3

Someone says to you:

> *"Nothing personal, but we don't know you. What makes you think you can run this meeting?"*

Wrong thing to say:

> *"I have a master's degree in organization development and this is exactly the sort of work I've been doing for 10 years. Besides, I've been hired by the director of this division to run this meeting."*

Right approach for handling resistance:

> **A.** *"I can understand that you might have reservations about my role today, since you don't know me. Can you elaborate a bit on what those specific concerns might be?"*

> **B.** *"I want to be an effective facilitator at this meeting. Can you tell me what would make you leave here saying that I had made a valuable contribution?"*

The Right Approach for Dealing with Resistance

The right approach for handling resistance always consists of two steps:

Step #1: Invite the resistor to express his or her resistance while you listen actively, paraphrase and offer empathy.
> *"Tell me why you feel this way?"*
> *"What happened last time?"*
> *"What are all of the things that are making you resist?"*

Step #2: After all the concerns have been acknowledged, ask questions to prompt the resistor to suggest solutions to the barriers.
> *"What circumstances would make you willing to stay?"*
> *"What assurance will eliminate your concerns?"*
> *"What supports will enable you to continue?"*

Why This Approach Works

Taking a facilitative or questioning approach works because the resistor is allowed to vent his or her frustration and be heard. The person is then consulted about what to do next. Since people do not generally refuse to act on their own suggestions, most people will then abandon their resistance and move forward.

Using the "wrong" approach doesn't work because it's a defensive response. You are basically telling people they have to comply. This stance usually makes people more angry and heightens their resistance.

Remember: Never get defensive... When you are defenseless you are invincible!

Every day, meeting leaders handle resistance incorrectly by telling people they have no choice and to "just get on with it." The problem with using this kind of force to blast through resistance is that it erodes people's commitment. They'll comply, but they won't give it their best effort or most creative ideas. That's why choosing the facilitative "ask approach" is always superior to the directive "tell style" when dealing with resistance. Another important reason for using the "ask" approach is that facilitators don't usually have power and control over the groups they're leading. When you have no control over people, ordering them to do something they don't want to do usually doesn't work.

Confrontational Facilitation

There are lots of times when a facilitator knows that group members are being polite while the "real" issues remain unspoken. While facilitation isn't a confrontational activity most of the time, there are situations in which you'll make the greatest contribution to the group by pushing members beyond their comfort zone. Sometimes clients will even ask to be pushed. They might say "we need to face our problems" or "force us to look at our deficiencies" or "don't let us get away with easy answers." In these situations, you're missing the boat by standing by quietly.

Confrontational facilitation isn't for beginners. Confronting people to get them to move out of their comfort zone or challenging traditional boundaries is for more advanced practitioners who can handle any conflict that might emerge. You have to be ready to make interventions and facilitate assertively if participant behaviors deteriorate.

Assuming an assertive stance also requires that you carefully set up the right norms and make sure it's acceptable to participants that you become more confrontational. This involves getting the members' permission to challenge their ideas and/or helping them determine acceptable boundaries for confrontation.

Once the right norms are in place and the group understands what you're doing, you can try any of the following techniques to apply pressure:

- Start off the session by asking a sequence of challenging questions designed to raise issues and create discontent with the present situation. (Refer to page 153 for details of the Sequential Questioning Technique.)

- Divide members into subgroups of two to three people to explore the most contentious issues and generate solutions. Share these solutions with the entire group. Post the best ideas and keep reminding members to act on them.

- At the mid-way point in the session (i.e. before they go off on a break or lunch) post a survey to help the group assess the session so far. Share the outcome and discuss what can be done about any low ratings. Use the following format:

Sometimes you have to push. Make people look over the edge and try something totally new!

1. We are really making meaningful progress.

1	2	3	4	5
definitely not!		not sure		absolutely!

2. We are dealing with the right issues.

1	2	3	4	5
definitely not!		not sure		absolutely!

3. We are being totally honest and open.

1	2	3	4	5
definitely not!		not sure		absolutely!

4. Our solutions are really innovative and will generate major improvements.

1	2	3	4	5
definitely not!		not sure		Absolutely!

- Just when people feel satisfied that they have good answers, challenge them to think of two or three alternative solutions for the same situation.
- Get people to put on other hats. Ask them what they would do if they owned the company, if they were the customer, if they were the shareholder, if they were the mailroom clerk, etc. Rotate hats to different people or groups in the room.
- Use silence to your advantage. Expect and accept that there may be awkwardness or heavy silence associated with any confrontation. Don't let this throw you off. Identify the silence by letting it stand until someone breaks it with a suggestion.

  > *"I'm sensing we have hit a nerve. Let's sit and think for a minute until someone comes up with a suggestion."*

- In some situations you may even have to issue a direct challenge. Announce that you don't think they're really getting to the truth or good solutions. Tell them that they need to dig deeper. Make a speech about what it takes to thrive in today's world. Give them a pep talk about how they need to do better.

If the feelings in the room are so sensitive that no one is willing to say anything, break people into subgroups of two or three members to discuss the current situation and generate solutions. Once you sense the group's initial unease has passed, reconvene the group and focus on solutions using the subgroup's ideas.

All experienced facilitators have stories about meetings where the discussion was purely superficial until they confronted the group. It's a sad truth that some meetings only get meaningful after people have been confronted and forced to face the facts. The more experienced you are, the more intolerant you'll become with discussions that waste people's valuable time, and the more ready you'll be to use confrontational methods. Never take confronting lightly. Make sure the approach fits the situation and is well timed. Most importantly, never do something simply to make yourself feel powerful or look smart.

When done right, a confrontation is often the very thing that will save a meeting from being a total waste of time.

Common Facilitation Dilemmas

Regardless of how well a session is prepared, there are always things that can go wrong. The following are common facilitation dilemmas and strategies that can help.

Scenario #1: *The group resists being facilitated*

The group desperately needs structure for its discussions, but doesn't like following a step-by-step process. They insist they don't want a facilitator. Members say it feels too formal. Sometimes there's a controlling chairperson present and he or she rejects the idea of having a formal facilitator.

Strategy: Facilitate from your seat at the side of the table. At appropriate moments, offer the group methods for tackling parts of the discussion. Informally act as timekeeper. Facilitate the discussion innocuously: ask questions, paraphrase, synthesize ideas and include quiet people, just as if you were up at the front of the room. Make notes on regular paper and offer your summaries when they're appropriate.

Potential facilitator mistake: Accepting that the group doesn't want process help and letting it flounder. While it's always best to be able to "officially" facilitate, it's possible to help a group by covertly playing the process role. Some attention to process is better than none.

Scenario #2: *Early in the meeting it appears the original agenda is wrong*

In spite of data gathering and proper planning, it becomes clear that the entire premise for the meeting is wrong. The group legitimately needs to discuss something else.

Strategy: Stop the meeting and verify your assessment that the existing agenda is now redundant. Take time to do agenda building. Ask members what they want to achieve at this session. Prioritize the issues and assign times. Take a fifteen minute break to regroup and create a new process design. Ratify the new agenda with the members. Be flexible and stay focused on the needs of the group.

Potential facilitator mistake: Force the group to follow the original agenda because of the energy and preparation that went into creating the design.

Scenario #3: *The meeting goes hopelessly off track*

Members are usually good at staying focused but have now gone totally off track and refuse to return to the planned agenda.

Strategy: Stop the off-topic discussion and determine whether members are aware that they're off topic and if they're comfortable with this. If they decide they want to stay with this new topic, help them structure their discussion. Ask:

> *"How long do you want to devote to this? What's the goal of this new discussion? What tools or methods should we use? etc."*

You should then facilitate the new discussion. If at any point they decide to return to the original agenda, "park" the current discussion and return to it at the end of the meeting to determine what should be done with it.

Always expect that things can go wrong!

Potential facilitator mistake: Stepping down from the facilitator role because the group isn't following the planned agenda or allowing the group to have a lengthy off-topic discussion in an unstructured manner. Trying to force the group back on topic when members feel a pressing need to discuss something else creates unnecessary conflict.

Scenario #4: *Group members ignore the process they originally agreed on*

There is a clear process for the session, but the members simply ignore it. When you attempt to get people to follow the agreed method, they revert to random discussion.

Strategy: Let them go on this way for a while, then ask: "How's this going? Are we getting anywhere?" Once a group has recognized that it isn't making progress, members are often ready to accept a more structured approach.

Potential facilitator mistake: Give up and stop watching for an opening to step back in and offer structure. Take an "I told you so" attitude if members admit frustration with their approach.

Scenario #5: *The group ignores its own norms*

Members have set clear behavioral norms, but start acting in ways that break all of their own rules.

Strategy: Allow them to be dysfunctional for a while, then ask:

> *"How do you feel this meeting is going in terms of the rules we set?"*
> *"Why do you think it's so hard sticking to the rules?"*
> *"How can we make sure we follow the rules?"*

Implement member suggestions. If they don't suggest anything, recommend that one or two group members be in charge of calling the group's attention to the rules any time they're being ignored or broken. This puts the onus on members to police themselves.

Potential facilitator mistake: Make all the interventions yourself and fail to use peer pressure to manage behavior.

Scenario #6: *People use the session to unload emotional baggage*

The agenda is swept off the table as people start venting their frustrations about their job, other people or the organization.

Strategy: Often groups can't focus on the task at hand because of pent-up feelings that have not been dealt with or recognized. In these cases it's healthy to encourage participants to release feelings by getting them out into the open. The key is to structure the venting so that it can be managed, and the feelings can be channeled into appropriate actions.

Some useful questions for managing venting sessions include:

"How important is it that we share these feelings now?"

"Do we need to have any rules (safety norms) about how we do this?"

"How long do we do it?"

"Are any of these issues problems we can solve?"

"What can we do to solve these problems?"

Potential facilitator mistake: Trying to suppress the venting process or letting it happen without any structure.

Scenario #7: *No matter what techniques are used, no decision is reached*

The group has been discussing options for hours and no clear decision is emerging. The discussion is spinning in circles and precious time is being wasted.

Strategy: Stop the action and look at the decision method that is being used. There are many decisions that simply cannot be made through consensus or voting. Consider using another method like a decision grid (see page 162) that allows for a comparative rating of individual aspects of competing options.

Another approach is to analyze the blocks to making a final decision. Ask: "What are all the things that are keeping us from making a decision?" List these and spend some time removing these decision barriers.

Potential facilitator mistake: Letting the group spin around for the entire meeting without checking the decision method and/or examining the decision barriers.

Scenario #8: *Members refuse to report back their discussions*

After a small group discussion, no one is willing to come forward and present the subgroup's ideas back to the larger group. There's a real concern that one or several of the ideas are too sensitive and that there might be repercussions.

Strategies: Divide the presentation and have two to three members from each group share the spotlight. If there's much material, the whole team can present portions back to the larger group. Also set the stage with the larger group by asking them to listen with an open mind and not react negatively to the presentation before having explored its potential.

Potential facilitator mistake: Taking the burden from the members and speaking for them. This shifts responsibility for the recommendations from members to yourself, and can result in members taking little responsibility for follow-up actions.

Scenario #9: *Members balk at assuming any responsibility for action plans*

People love discussing problems and brainstorming ideas, but when it comes to action planning, everyone is suddenly too busy or insecure about his or her ability to complete the task.

Strategy: Ensure that it's clear from the start that any problem-solving exercise includes action planning and that members will be expected to assume major responsibility for implementing their ideas.

Implementing action plans is often a growth activity if people can be given support and encouragement to stretch beyond their present capabilities. When people are concerned that they can't succeed, ask them: "What help, training, and/or other supports do you need?" Work to provide those enabling resources.

If members have time barriers to participating in implementation, these need to be identified and problem solved. Organizations often ask the same hardworking people to be on every committee. If there's any control over who is going to be asked to work on an activity, considerable thought should be given to whether these individuals have the time needed to devote to the activity.

Potential facilitator mistake: Let people "off the hook" too easily by not problem solving the blocks or letting the same people shoulder all of the work. The worst strategy of all is to take responsibility for the action steps yourself.

Collaborative conflict management is essentially consensus decision making.

The Collaborative Conflict Management Process

The steps in managing differences of opinion collaboratively are essentially the same ones outlined in detail on pages 123 to 131 in the chapter on decision making. Once the emotions surrounding the situation have been vented, managing conflict collaboratively involves:

Step #1: *Clarify the issue* – create a clear statement of what the issue is. Ensure that everyone agrees with that statement.

Step #2: *Identify the desired outcome* – help the members create a goal statement that describes what the situation would look like if the issue were resolved.

Step #3: *Set a time frame* – set strict time limits and keep to them.

Step #4: *Make sure appropriate norms are in place* – if things are likely to get emotional, make sure the team has targeted norms for conflict situations.

Step #5: *Explain the collaborative/consensual process to be used* - emphasize the need to analyze objectively before jumping to solutions.

Step #6: *Analyze the facts of the situation* – make sure everyone is heard and that an objective exploration of the current situation is carried out.

Step #7: *Generate a range of possible solutions* – use participative techniques like brainstorming (see Chapter 8).

Step #8: *Evaluate the solutions* – use a decision grid (page 162) and establish objective criteria for finding the best solution.

Step #9: *Plan to implement the agreed to solutions* – make sure that the what, how, who and when are specified. Troubleshoot the action plan to make sure the steps are doable.

Use this sheet when you wish to provide detailed feedback to two people interacting during conflict.

Observing Interpersonal Conflict Worksheet

Behaviors that help	Person "A"	Person "B"
1. Leaning forward – listening actively		
2. Paraphrasing – "Is this what you're saying?"		
3. Questioning to clarify – "Let me understand this better."		
4. Showing respect to the other's opinion– valuing input		
5. Calmness – voice tone low, relaxed body posture		
6. Open and vulnerable – showing flexibility		
7. Clearly stating my position – assertive stance		
8. Checking for agreement on what is to be resolved		
9. Laying out ground rules – "What will help us?"		
10. Showing empathy – checking perceptions		
11. "I" statements – disclosing feelings		
12. Using other person's name		
13. Body contact – if appropriate		
14. Problem solving – looking at alternatives		
15. Win/win attitude – concern for other person		
16. Congruence – between verbal and non-verbal behavior		
17. Concern for other person's goal		
18. Feedback – giving specific descriptive details		

Behaviors that hinder	Person "A"	Person "B"
1. Interrupting		
2. Showing disrespect		
3. Entrapment questions		
4. Talking too much		
5. Pushing for solution		
6. Arguing about personal perception		
7. Aggressive manner		
8. Accusing, laying blame		
9. Smirking, getting personal		
10. "You made me" statements		
11. Non-receptive to suggestions		
12. Not identifying real feelings		
13. Ending before finishing		
14. Incongruity of words and actions		
15. Defensiveness		
16. Denying, not owning problems		
17. Blocking, talking off-topic – changing the subject		
18. Not giving specific feedback		

Use this observation sheet when you want to give feedback to a group about how members handled conflict.

Group Conflict Checklist

	Comments
No plan or process for approaching the task Group wanders from one topic to another because there's no format for discussion. No time is taken at the start of the meeting to set up parameters.	
Lack of active listening Instead of acknowledging each other's points before making their own, people push their own ideas in a totally unconnected sequence.	
Lack of closure The group moves from one topic to another without discussing the merits of previous ideas.	
Personal attacks People use a sarcastic tone, ignore each other, interrupt or even attack each other. They don't focus on the facts.	
No process checking The group forges ahead without ever stopping to discuss whether the process is working or requires modification.	
Dominant members A few people do all the talking. No one notices or even cares that some people are left out.	
Poor time management Time isn't budgeted or monitored. Time is wasted on the wrong things.	
Folding People just give in when things get rough. They don't systematically follow issues through.	
Lack of skill Members don't possess any tools for making decisions. They also lack important interpersonal skills.	
Passive or nonexistent facilitation No one is providing order or policing the action. No notes are kept. Everyone is taking sides. If there's a facilitator, he or she is unwilling to offer procedural options or keep order.	

Group members can use this checklist for observing and giving feedback to you (or other facilitators) at the end of a session.

Conflict Management Observation Sheet

Instructions:

Observe the facilitator to see which of the following he or she does. Make note of as many specific incidents as possible to enrich the feedback.

Behaviors that Help	Behaviors that Hinder
__ letting people vent	__ arguing
__ asking for dissenting views	__ defensiveness
__ paraphrasing a lot	__ asking entrapping questions
__ showing respect for opposing views	__ letting a few people dominate
__ eye contact	__ favoring one side of any debate
__ effective body language	__ letting it get emotional or personal
__ calmness	__ ending before resolution
__ non-defensiveness	__ sidestepping the really hot issues
__ validating speakers	__ not using a process
__ redirecting sarcasm	__ not using the norms
__ confronting the facts	__ lack of empathy for member feelings
__ taking a problem-solving approach	__ letting it drag on
__ using norms for control	
__ showing concern for others' feelings	
__ making interventions	
__ checking on how people are doing	
__ disclosing personal feelings	
__ ensuring a good decision is made	
__ bringing proper closure	
__ mediating conflicts between two people	
__ making sure everyone stays involved	
__ evaluating how the team did during the conflict to learn from mistakes	

If you want to help a team in conflict understand exactly what's going on, use this survey to surface specific problems. (Refer to page 193 for the details of managing survey feedback.)

 Conflict Effectiveness Survey

Read over the following statements and rate how your group currently manages conflict. Be totally honest. Remember that this survey is anonymous. The results will be tabulated, and results will be fed back to the group for assessment.

1. Listening

1	2	3	4	5	6	7

People assume they're right   People are open to hearing new ideas

2. Acknowledging

1	2	3	4	5	6	7

People put their ideas on the table without acknowledging the points made by others   People acknowledge each other's ideas even when they don't agree with them

3. Objectivity

1	2	3	4	5	6	7

We tend to get emotional and argue for our favorite ideas   We tend to stay calm and look objectively at the facts

4. Building

1	2	3	4	5	6	7

We tend not to admit that anyone else's ideas are good   We generally take the ideas of fellow members and try to build on them

5. Norms

1	2	3	4	5	6	7

We don't have or use norms to manage conflict situations   We have created a good set of norms that work well to help us manage conflicts

6. Trust and Openness

1	2	3	4	5	6	7

People don't say what's really on their minds   There is a lot of trust that you can say whatever you have on your mind

Conflict Effectiveness Survey, cont'd

7. Approach to Conflict

| 1 | 2 | 3 | 4 | 5 | 6 | 7 |

Most often we either avoid
or argue vehemently

We tend to collaborate
to find solutions we
can all live with

8. Interpersonal Behaviors

| 1 | 2 | 3 | 4 | 5 | 6 | 7 |

People often get emotional
and make personal attacks

We stay calm and stick to
the facts. No one ever
gets personally attacked

9. Structure

| 1 | 2 | 3 | 4 | 5 | 6 | 7 |

We never take a systematic approach.
Mostly we just thrash out differences

There is always a clearly defined
process for analyzing the situation
& looking for solutions

10. Closure

| 1 | 2 | 3 | 4 | 5 | 6 | 7 |

Most of our conflict sessions
end without resolution

We are excellent at getting
to solutions and clear action steps

11. Process Checking

| 1 | 2 | 3 | 4 | 5 | 6 | 7 |

Once an argument starts
we never call time-out and correct ourselves

We always stop and take
a look at how we are managing
our conflicts so we can improve

12. Time Management

| 1 | 2 | 3 | 4 | 5 | 6 | 7 |

When things get heated we
lose all track of time and our
agenda goes out the window

We very carefully monitor our
time to make sure we aren't wasting
it, especially when we get into conflict

13. Aftermath

| 1 | 2 | 3 | 4 | 5 | 6 | 7 |

People are usually angry
for a long time afterward

We work at clearing
the air of hurt feelings

✎ *Notes*

_____

_____

_____

_____

_____

_____

_____

_____

_____

_____

_____

_____

_____

_____

_____

_____

_____

_____

_____

_____

_____

_____

Chapter 6
Effective Decision Making

Helping groups make high-quality decisions is the most important function of a facilitator. Unfortunately, decision making is also one of the most difficult things to do properly.

Picture yourself facilitating the third meeting in a row where the same hot issue gets thrashed around without a final decision. Once again three people do all the talking while all others squirm or excuse themselves and leave. This decision has to finally be made. How are you going to do it?

First, attune yourself to some typical scenarios that illustrate a poor decision process:

- several members of the group have tuned out as the discussion enters its second half hour of floating aimlessly, with no resolution in sight
- when the big decision finally comes to the table, there is little time left in the meeting so there's only a brief discussion of the key points, followed by a show of hands to arrive at an agreement
- two of the team's members have little to say during a lengthy discussion, but later complain to teammates about not being asked their opinions
- after an hour of talking, no real decision has been reached, so discussion moves on to another topic
- instead of debating ideas, the discussion seems more like a clash of wills, as members battle it out to see who can win over the others
- even though they hold strong views, people start to fold or give in, just to get it over with
- after the meeting is over, several people are overheard complaining that they can't really support the decision that was made

If any of these sound familiar, you may be working with a group that needs to learn to become more effective at making decisions.

Helping groups make high-quality decisions is the most important function of a facilitator.

Symptoms, Causes and Cures of Poor Decisions

When groups make poor-quality decisions, one or more of the following symptoms are likely taking place:

Symptom #1:   Aimless drifting and random discussions.

The same topic gets kicked around meeting after meeting without resolution. Feels like the group is spinning its wheels.

Cause: No plan or process for approaching the decision

Group members simply launch into the discussion without any thought to which tools to use. Without a systematic approach, people start proposing solutions before there has been a thorough analysis of the situation. There is a lack of proper information. Everyone puts his or her favorite solution on the table. No one takes notes. No solution is ever definitively agreed to. Detailed action plans aren't written down.

Cure: The group needs a structured approach to decision making that uses the right decision-making tool and is assertively facilitated.

Symptom #2: **The group uses voting on important items where total buy-in is important, then uses consensus to decide trivial issues.**

Cause: A lack of understanding decision-making options.

The group doesn't understand what the six key decision-making tools are and when to use them.

Cure: The group needs to be familiar with the six main decision-making options and consciously decide which to use before launching into any decision-making discussion. (refer to pages 115 to 117.)

Symptom #3: **The group always seems to run out of time just when the important decisions get onto the table.**

Cause: Poor time management

Time isn't budgeted or monitored. There's no detailed agenda that sets aside the time needed to deal with important items. Hence, time is wasted discussing unimportant items. Meetings often start/run late.

Cure: The group needs to create a detailed agenda before each meeting. At the meeting the facilitator needs to be assertive about staying on track and on time.

Symptom #4: **When an important item is on the table, people get heated and argumentative. No one really listens to the opposing viewpoints. Everyone just pushes his or her point and tries to be right. Some members dominate, unconcerned that others are silent.**

Cause: Poorly developed group interaction skills

No one is really listening to each other's points, just pushing his or her own. No one knows how to structure a decision-making session. Facilitation is nonexistent or weak. As a result there's an absence of the synergy you get when people build on each other's ideas. This confrontational style strains relationships, which only makes things worse.

Cure: The members need training in group effectiveness skills so that they can exhibit more listening, supporting and idea building. This can be through a formal team training session or through informal practice sessions interjected into their meetings. A training plan to teach members to be effective is included on page 79.

Symptom #5: **After a lengthy discussion, it becomes clear that everyone is operating on slightly different assumptions about what the problem is and what the constraints or possibilities are.**

Cause: Failure to check assumptions

Everyone has a different view of the situation and is basing his or her input on that view. Assumptions are never put on the table for sharing or testing.

Cure: Use probing questions to uncover the assumptions underlying statements made by the members. These questions can be related to the situation, the organization or the people involved. Once the assumptions are on the table, they can be tested and validated or eliminated. Members will then be operating within the same framework.

Symptom #6: **In spite of the fact that the discussion has been going in circles for some time, no one takes action to get things back on track.**

Cause: No process checking

Even when things are going nowhere and frustration levels are running high, no one knows to call time-out to take stock and regroup. This, once again, reflects the absence of facilitation.

Cure: Stopping the discussion periodically to ask how things are going, whether the pace is right, whether people feel progress is being made, whether people feel the right approach is being taken. (Refer to the discussion of process checking on page 43.)

If you want to assess your group's current decision-making effectiveness, use the following checklist as a post-meeting survey or an observation sheet during a decision-making session. Feed back the data collected once the survey results have been tabulated. (Refer to the process outlined on page 193.)

Decision-Making Survey

1	2	3	4	5
Clear step-by-step process used | | | | Lack of systematic planned approach

1	2	3	4	5
Thorough checking of assumptions | | | | No checking of assumptions

1	2	3	4	5
Use of the right decision method | | | | Overuse voting, misuse consensus

1	2	3	4	5
Active listening by members | | | | No one builds on the ideas of others

1	2	3	4	5
People build on each other's ideas | | | | People focus on their own ideas

1	2	3	4	5
Objectively debate ideas | | | | Emotionally argue points of view

1	2	3	4	5
Periodic process checking | | | | Never stopping to check

1	2	3	4	5
Time carefully managed | | | | Use of time isn't planned

1	2	3	4	5
Active and assertive facilitation | | | | Passive or lack of facilitation

1	2	3	4	5
Full and equal participation | | | | Some dominate, others are passive

1	2	3	4	5
True closure | | | | Little gets decided

1	2	3	4	5
Clear action plans | | | | No plans to implement

The Six Decision-Making Options

As a facilitator you have six distinct decision-making methods available. Each of these options represents a different approach. Each has pros and cons associated with it. The decision option should always be chosen carefully to be sure it's the most appropriate method for the decision that's before the group. These six options are (in reverse order of their relative value):

Option #6: Spontaneous Agreement

This happens occasionally when there's a solution that is favored by everyone and 100 percent agreement seems to happen automatically. These types of decisions are usually made quickly and automatically. They are fairly rare and often occur in connection with the more trivial or simple issues.

Pros – it's fast, easy, everyone is happy, it unites the group.

Cons – may be too fast; perhaps the issue actually needed discussion.

Uses – when lack of discussion isn't vital (i.e. issues are trivial); or when issues are not complex, requiring no in-depth discussion.

Be wary of spontaneous agreement for making important decisions.

Option #5: One person decides

This is a decision that the group decides to refer to one person to make on behalf of the group. A common misconception among teams is that every decision needs to be made by the whole group. In fact, a one-person decision is often a faster and more efficient way to get resolution. The quality of any one person's decision can be raised considerably if the person making the decision gets advice and input from other group members before deciding.

Pros – it's fast and accountability is clear. Can result in commitment and buy-in if people feel their ideas are represented.

Cons – it can divide the group if the person deciding doesn't consult, or makes a decision that others can't live with. A one-person decision typically lacks in both the buy-in and synergy that come from a group decision-making process.

Uses – when the issue is unimportant or small; or when there's a clear expert in the group; or when only one person has the information needed to make the decision and can't share it; or when one person is solely accountable for the outcome.

Many groups ignore the fact that many decisions are best made by one person.

Option #4: Compromise

A negotiated approach is applicable when there are two or more distinct options and members are strongly polarized (neither side is willing to accept the solution/ position put forth by the other side). A middle position is then created that incorporates ideas from both sides. Throughout the process of negotiation, everyone wins a few favorite points, but also loses a few items he or she liked. The outcome is, therefore, something that no one is totally satisfied with. In compromises no one feels he or she got what he or she originally wanted, so the emotional reaction is often "It's not really what I wanted, but I'm going to have to live with it."

A compromise creates feelings of both win and lose.

Pros – it generates lots of discussion and does create a solution.

Cons – negotiating when people are pushing a favored point of view tends to be adversarial, hence this approach divides the group. In the end everyone wins, but everyone also loses.

Uses – when two opposing solutions are proposed, neither of which are acceptable to everyone; or when the group is strongly polarized and compromise is the only alternative.

Option #3: Multi-voting

This is a priority-setting tool that is useful for making decisions when the group has a lengthy set of options and rank ordering the options, based on a set of criteria, will clarify the best course of action. (Refer to page 159).

Pros – it's systematic, objective, democratic, non-competitive, and participative. Everyone wins somewhat, and feelings of loss are minimal. It's a fast way of sorting out a complex set of options. Often feels consensual.

Cons – it's often associated with limited discussion, hence, limited understanding of the options. This may force choices on people that may not be satisfactory to them, because the real priorities do not rise to the surface or people are swayed by each other if the voting is done out in the open, rather than electronically or by ballot.

Uses – when there's a long list of alternatives or items from which to choose or when choosing a set of criteria to identify the best course of action.

Option #2: Majority Voting

This involves asking people to choose the option they favor, once clear choices have been identified. Usual methods are a show of hands or secret ballot. The quality of voting is always enhanced if there's good discussion to share ideas before the vote is taken.

Pros – it's fast and decisions can be of higher quality if the vote is preceded by a thorough analysis.

Cons – it can be too fast and low in quality if people vote based on their personal feelings without the benefit of hearing each other's thoughts or facts. It creates winners and losers, hence dividing the group. The show of hands method may put pressure on people to conform.

Uses – when there are two distinct options and one or the other must be chosen; when decisions must be made quickly, and a division in the group is acceptable. When consensus has been attempted and can't be reached.

Option #1: Consensus Building

Involves everyone clearly understanding the situation or problem to be decided, analyzing all of the relevant facts together and then jointly developing solutions that represent the whole group's best thinking about the optimal decision. It's char-

Multi-voting is a good tool if there are a lot of options or a lot of people involved.

The quality of any voting exercise increases dramatically if it's preceded by a thorough discussion.

acterized by a lot of listening, healthy debate and testing of options. Consensus generates a decision about which everyone says, "I can live with it."

Pros – it's a collaborative effort that unites the group. It demands high involvement. It's systematic, objective and fact-driven. It builds buy-in and high commitment to the outcome.

Cons – it's time-consuming and produces low-quality decisions if done without proper data collection or if members have poor interpersonal skills.

Uses – when decisions will impact the entire group; when buy-in and ideas from all members are essential; when the importance of the decision being made is worth the time it will take to complete the consensus process properly.

Remember that each option has its place, so choose the most appropriate method before each decision-making session.

Consensus building creates participation and "buy-in" to the generated solutions.

Decision Options Chart			
Option	**Pros**	**Cons**	**Uses**
Spontaneous Agreement	• fast, easy • unites	• too fast • lack of discussion	• when full discussion isn't critical • trivial issues
One Person	• can be fast • clear accountability	• lack of input • low buy-in • no synergy	• when one person is the expert • individual willing to take sole responsibility
Compromise	• discussion • creates a solution	• adversarial • win/lose • divides the group	• when positions are polarized; concensus improbable
Multi-voting	• systematic • objective • participative • feels like a win	• limits dialogue • influenced choices • real priorities may not surface	• to sort or prioritize a long list of options
Voting	• fast • high quality with dialogue • clear outcome	• may be too fast • winners and losers • no dialogue • influenced choices	• trivial matter • when there are clear options • if division of group is OK
Consensus Building	• collaborative • systematic • participative • discussion-oriented • encourages commitment	• takes time • requires data and member skills	• important issues • when total buy-in matters

Understanding Consensus

The crucial importance of consensus simply cannot be overstated and must be fully understood by all facilitators. In fact facilitation and consensus are based on the same set of core values and beliefs.

Besides being the #1 choice as a decision mode for all important decisions, facilitators are constantly building consensus with everything they do.

The following are all examples of consensus activities:

- Summarizing a complex set of ideas to the satisfaction of group members
- Getting everyone's input into a clear goal and objectives for the group's activities
- Gaining buy-in from all members as to the purpose of the session
- Linking people's ideas together so they feel they're saying the same thing
- Making notes on a flip chart in such a way that at the end of the discussion each member sees where and how they've contributed and is satisfied with what has been recorded
- Discussing and agreeing on which decision mode to use in a formal decision-making process.

Because all facilitation activities must strive to be collaborative, participative, synergistic and unifying, all facilitation activities are essentially consensus building in nature!

Hallmarks of the Consensus Process

Regardless of whether consensus is being used formally to reach a decision on a specific issue, or informally as an ongoing facilitation technique, you know the group is working consensually if:

- there are lots of ideas being shared
- people's feelings are openly explored
- everyone's heard
- there's active listening and paraphrasing to clarify ideas, and ideas are built on by other members
- no one's trying to push a pre-determined solution; instead there's an open and objective quest for new options
- the final solution is based on sound information
- when the final solution is reached, people feel satisfied that they were part of the decision
- everyone feels so consulted and involved that even though the final solution isn't the one they would have chosen working on their own, they can readily "live with it."

There are many situations in which the decisions being made are of such magnitude that consensus needs to be designated as the only acceptable method of decision making. In these cases, the group agrees to keep discussing until everyone indicates that he or she can live with the outcome.

Defaulting to voting (or any other technique that creates division within the group) for sensitive decisions allows dissenters to absolve themselves of responsibility for important group outcomes.

If the whole-hearted commitment of all members is important to a particular decision, facilitators need to use the strategies for overcoming resistance outlined on page 98.

This involves openly asking resistors:

1.) What stops you from supporting this idea?
What are your specific objections?

2.) What changes, amendments or additions would make this an idea you could live with?

One of the major contributions of any facilitator is in helping a group overcome the temptation to "pressure" dissenters into agreement. By openly accepting and discussing differences, facilitators help members reach decisions that have been objectively explored and tested.

You shouldn't end a consensus exercise by asking "Is everyone happy?" or even "Does everyone agree?" At the end of even a great consensus process, people have usually made concessions, and are likely not getting everything they "wanted."

Consensus isn't designed to make people happy or leave them in 100 percent agreement. Its goal is to create an outcome that represents the best feasible course of action given the circumstances.

Some decisions are so important that only consensus will do.

Don't ask
"Do we all agree?"
OR
"Is everyone happy?"

Instead ask
"Have we got a well-thought-through outcome that we can all feel committed to implementing, and that everyone can live with?"

Things to Watch for in Decision Making

Decision making is rarely easy. The following are some extra tips to help you manage decision-making sessions.

 ___ Be clear on the process to be used right up-front. Explain any tools or techniques that will be used.

___ Ask people what assumptions they're operating under, either about the issue or the organizational constraints. Note these and test them with the rest of the group.

___ Conflict is a natural part of many decision-making discussions. Always confront differences assertively and collaboratively. Don't strive to avoid conflict or accommodate by asking people to be nice and get along.

___ Urge people not to fold or just give in if they feel they have important ideas. When everyone agrees just to make things run smoothly, the result is "group think." This creates poor decisions made just to get it over with and ensure that everyone stays friends.

___ If the group has chosen to go for consensus because the issue is important, stick with it even if the going gets tough. Beware of the tendency to start voting, coin tossing, and bargaining to make things easier.

___ Be very particular about achieving closure on any items that get decided. Test for consensus and make sure things are final before letting the group move on to other topics.

___ Stop the action if things start "spinning" or behaviors get ineffective. Ask: "What are we doing well? What aren't we doing so well?" and "What do we need to do about it?" Then act on the suggestions for improvement.

Effective Decision-Making Behaviors

To make any decision process work, group members need to behave themselves in specific ways. These behaviors can be suggested to the group or generated as norms in advance of any decision-making session.

Behaviors that Help	Behaviors that Hinder
Listening to other's ideas politely, even when you don't agree	Interrupting people in mid-sentence
Paraphrasing the main points made by another person, especially if you're about to contradict the person's ideas	Not acknowledging the ideas that others have put on the table
Praising others' ideas	Criticizing others' ideas, as opposed to giving them useful feedback
Building on others' ideas	Pushing your own ideas while ignoring others' input
Asking others to critique your ideas, and accepting the feedback	Getting defensive when your ideas are analyzed
Being open to accepting alternative courses of action	Sticking only to your ideas and blocking suggestions for alternatives
Dealing with facts	Basing arguments on feelings
Staying calm and friendly toward colleagues	Getting overly emotional; showing hostility in the face of any disagreement

Shifting Decision-Making Paradigms

The use of facilitation creates a "paradigm shift."

You need to be aware that when organizations start using groups to make decisions that were formerly made by managers, this often represents a major shift in the power arrangements and cultural values of the whole organization.

Many managers are used to listening to input and then making all of the important decisions themselves. Such patterns are a reality that all facilitators need to be aware of. In these situations, the use of consensus or majority voting to make decisions could represent a major cultural shift. Sensitivity is needed to help both leaders and members understand the value of participative decisions, and to create the right setting in which people can be encouraged to express their ideas freely.

When working with a group you don't know, never assume that participative decision making is understood or practised by either the group or leader.

Instead, check by asking questions that probe how the organization normally makes decisions: are member decisions often overturned by leaders? or are groups normally empowered to make important decisions?

Leaders who are accustomed to the old way of doing things often fear losing total control by handing a meeting over to a facilitator. These leaders need to buy into the value of member participation in decision making. They also need to understand how this power shift opens the door for them to play new roles.

Some points that may be helpful in persuading a leader to respect and accept group decisions include:

- group decision making has the benefits of getting more ideas, building commitment, and getting members to take greater responsibility for implementing actions

- "risky" decisions can be handled so that members only get to offer ideas or make recommendations. In these cases the leader still has control over the final approval of the outcome (empowerment level III)

- decisions that group members are empowered to make without needing final approval can be given clear parameters to ensure they meet key success criteria, such as: compliance with budgetary guidelines, support of the overall strategic plan, etc.

- group decision making takes some of the "monkeys" off the leader's back and lets him or her play the roles of valued member of the group, expert resource, or project sponsor

Help controlling leaders get comfortable with group decisions.

If the leader remains concerned about a participative decision process, you'll need to get clarity about which specific decisions can be made by the group and which can't. The four-level empowerment chart (page 65) can be used to identify the level of decision-making power members will have on specific issues.

While facilitators can take part in sessions in which participants are only giving their ideas and have no decision-making powers (level II), it should be made clear that this isn't the full use of any group's powers.

The bottom line is that there has to be total clarity about which decisions can be made by members, and to what extent they'll be given management support for their suggestions. When parameters aren't specifically defined, group decisions are often overturned later on.

Overview of the Systematic Consensus-Building Process

When an <u>important</u> decision needs to be made, the following should take place:

Use a systematic process to make important consensus decisions.

- the matter to be decided is allocated a time slot on the agenda
- members are given ample time to do their homework and gather needed information
- a facilitator is chosen. He or she asks for someone to act as timekeeper
- the facilitator helps the group write a clear statement of the item that needs to be decided
- the facilitator gets the group to identify the "desired outcome" or goal of the discussion
- the facilitator makes sure that there are agreed-to norms in place
- the facilitator helps the group to decide which of the six decision types it will be using to make the final decision
- the facilitator explains the key steps so everyone understands the process
- the facilitator begins the discussion with a thorough analysis of the current situation. Assumptions are surfaced and tested.
- after a thorough analysis the group starts to generate possible solutions. All solution ideas are recorded
- throughout the proceedings, the facilitator checks periodically on whether members feel that progress is being made, that the pace is appropriate, that the process is working, etc.
- suggested solutions are then evaluated according to a set of criteria created by the group
- the final solution is agreed to and a clear course of action is laid out
- members work to create detailed action plans
- to ensure that nothing goes wrong, the team troubleshoots their action plan by anticipating all the reasons they may fail to implement key steps
- roles and responsibilities are specified and a reporting mechanism is designed
- as members leave the meeting, they help to evaluate how the meeting went by filling out a brief survey on the decision process

On the next several pages there are worksheets that provide structure for the process outlined above. Refer to the section on *Process Tools* (Chapter 8) for more in-depth descriptions of the various tools available for key steps.

Experienced facilitators will notice that this decision process is a modification of *Systematic Problem Solving* (Chapter 8). That's because systematic problem solving is a consensual process that provides a solid foundation for any work group seeking to resolve important issues. It's the most important tool in the facilitator's repertoire and should be taught to all groups.

Consensus Decision Worksheet

Use these steps systematically to provide structure to an important decision-making process:

Step 1. Write a clear decision statement
What is the item or issue that we'll be deciding on?

_____
_____
_____
_____
_____
_____
_____
_____
_____

Step 2. Identify the desired goal or outcome
How will we know that we have made an effective decision?

_____
_____
_____
_____
_____
_____
_____
_____
_____

Step 3. Set time frames
Indicate the time per each portion of the discussion:

Agenda Item	_Time Req'd_	_Presenter_

Total time required = _____

*Facilitation
Tools*

*Synthesize
member ideas.*

*Each person
writes down
goal statement
to share.*

Create a grid.

Synthesize ideas.

Step 4. Clarify Group Norms

What rules do we need to set for ourselves to ensure that we have a really participative and balanced debate instead of heated arguments?

_____
_____
_____
_____
_____
_____
_____
_____
_____
_____
_____
_____
_____
_____
_____
_____
_____
_____
_____

Clarify which portions of the discussion will require which decision mode.

Step 5. Identify the Decision-Making Process

How will we be making the ultimate decision?

consensus _____   majority voting _____

compromise _____   one person decides _____

unanimous _____   multi-voting _____

Comments:

_____
_____
_____
_____
_____
_____
_____
_____
_____
_____
_____
_____
_____
_____
_____
_____

Step 6. Analyze the Situation

Ask: *"What are all of the relevant facts that describe the background of the current situation surrounding this decision? What do we all need to understand?"* You also need to ask, *"What are the assumptions we are operating under? Which of these are valid? What other constraints, boundaries or political realities should we take into consideration?"*

_____
_____
_____
_____
_____
_____
_____
_____
_____
_____
_____
_____
_____
_____
_____
_____
_____
_____
_____
_____
_____
_____
_____
_____
_____
_____
_____
_____
_____
_____
_____
_____

Can use: cause/effect analysis; force-field analysis; questioning.

Step 7. Generate Possible Solutions

What are all of the possible solutions that might work given our analysis?

Can use: brain-storming, anonymous brainstorming.

_____

_____

_____

_____

_____

_____

_____

_____

_____

_____

_____

_____

_____

_____

_____

_____

_____

_____

_____

_____

_____

_____

_____

_____

_____

_____

_____

_____

_____

_____

_____

_____

_____

_____

_____

_____

_____

_____

Step 8. Evaluate Solutions Against Criteria

Ask: *"What criteria should we consider to help us sort through all of the possible solutions? Are all of the criteria equal in importance, or do we need to give some greater weight than others?"*

Examples of "criteria" include: *cost, impact, difficulty/ease, timeliness, urgency, match with priorities, customer need, innovative, cost reduction, impact on quality, employee satisfaction, health and safety, environmental impact, etc.*

Use the following *Criteria-Based Grid* to conduct the analysis:

Criteria (weight)	Solutions					
	#1	#2	#3	#4	#5	#6
____ ( )						
____ ( )						
____ ( )						
____ ( )						
Totals						

Can also use the impact/ effect grid.

How to rate:

Step 1 – rate how critical each criteria item is to the final decision. Use a scale of 1 to 3, where 1 = somewhat important, 2 = important, and 3 = critical

Step 2 – rate each solution on how well it meets each criteria item. Use a scale of 1 to 3, where 1 = poorly meets the criteria, 2 = somewhat meets the criteria, 3 = meets criteria very well

Step 3 – weight each solution by multiplying the two ratings together (created in *Steps 1 & 2*) for each criteria item. Add all the criteria weights for each solution to determine each solution's total weight

Outcome:

Indicate which solution(s) will be used to make action plans for implementation.

_____

_____

_____

_____

_____

_____

_____

Use synthesis.

Step 9. Action Planning

Indicate:

What will be done & how?	By whom?	By when?	Results indicator(s)?

Step 10. Troubleshoot the Action Plan

Ask:

What are all of the things that can get in the way of implementing our actions?	*What can we do about each of these possible blocks?*

Use group synthesis.

Use synthesis.

Step 11. Reporting on Progress

When will we meet to report back on any progress?

_____
_____
_____
_____
_____
_____
_____
_____
_____

How will we report back? (written, verbal)

_____
_____
_____
_____
_____
_____
_____
_____

What do we need to report on?

_____
_____
_____
_____
_____
_____
_____

Who else in the organization needs to be made aware of our decisions and action steps? How do we communicate with them?

_____
_____
_____
_____
_____
_____
_____
_____

Step 12. Evaluate the Decision Process

Anonymously provide your feedback on today's session.

1. Rate the thoroughness of our process.

1	2	3	4	5
Poor	Fair	Satisfactory	Good	Excellent

2. What is the quality of the final decision(s) made?

1	2	3	4	5
Poor	Fair	Satisfactory	Good	Excellent

3. How effective was today's use of our time?

1	2	3	4	5
Poor	Fair	Satisfactory	Good	Excellent

4. To what extent was true closure achieved?

1	2	3	4	5
Poor	Fair	Satisfactory	Good	Excellent

5. How doable are our action plans?

1	2	3	4	5
Poor	Fair	Satisfactory	Good	Excellent

6. How well did people do their homework?

1	2	3	4	5
Poor	Fair	Satisfactory	Good	Excellent

7. How good were we at really listening and building on each other's ideas?

1	2	3	4	5
Poor	Fair	Satisfactory	Good	Excellent

8. What is your level of satisfaction with the final decision?

1	2	3	4	5
Poor	Fair	Satisfactory	Good	Excellent

9. What would you do to improve our next decision-making session?

_____

_____

_____

_____

10. What feedback would you like to give to the facilitator?

_____

_____

_____

_____

Can use a survey or post a single exit survey.

✎ Notes

_____

_____

_____

_____

_____

_____

_____

_____

_____

_____

_____

_____

_____

_____

_____

_____

_____

_____

_____

_____

_____

_____

_____

Chapter 7
Meeting Management

"Oh no, not another meeting!!!"

*I*f you hear this every time a meeting is called, there may be some real meeting design issues that you need to address. As facilitator, it's your job to help others learn how to work effectively in order to achieve their goals.

Use the following checklist to pinpoint some of the common elements of ineffective meetings:

— some members not clear about the meeting goal
— a vague or nonexistent agenda
— no time limits on discussions
— no discernible process for working on important issues
— no one facilitating discussions
— people haven't done their homework
— discussions go in circles
— lack of closure to discussions
— people vehemently arguing points of view rather than debating ideas
— a few people dominating while others sit passively
— meetings that end without detailed action plans for agreed next steps
— absence of any process checking of the meeting as it unfolds
— no evaluation at the end

Meetings that Work

By contrast, here are the ingredients shared by all effective meetings:

— a detailed agenda that spells out what will be discussed, the goal of the discussion, who is bringing that item forward, and an estimate of how long each item will take
— clear process notes that describe the tools and techniques that will be used
— assigned roles such as facilitator, chairperson, minute taker, and timekeeper
— a set of group norms created by the members and posted in the meeting room
— clarity about decision-making options and how they will be used
— effective member behaviors
— periodic process checks to make sure progress is being made
— clear conflict-management strategies
— a process that creates true closure

133

— detailed and clear minutes

— specific follow-up plans

— a post-meeting evaluation

<u>Special Note</u>: *We've already discussed such factors as setting group norms, decision-making options, effective member behaviors, and conflict management in previous chapters, so we won't spend too much time on them here. In this chapter you'll learn about other factors (such as agenda design) that are essential to making meetings work.*

There are a number of symptoms of ineffective meetings. Once you learn to spot them, think of them as a set of early warning signals against which to periodically check how healthy your own meetings are.

You can use this questionnaire to assess the overall quality of past meetings. Then use the survey feedback method described on page 193 in Chapter 9.

Meeting Diagnostic Survey

1. People tend to resist the idea of another meeting.

1	2	3	4	5
Totally disagree	Disagree	Doesn't apply/ not sure	Agree	Totally agree

2. Meetings generally do not start or end on time.

1	2	3	4	5
Totally disagree	Disagree	Doesn't apply/ not sure	Agree	Totally agree

3. When a member offers an idea, other members do not ask detailed questions or demonstrate active listening.

1	2	3	4	5
Totally disagree	Disagree	Doesn't apply/ not sure	Agree	Totally agree

4. Discussions begin before it's clear to everyone exactly what is being discussed.

1	2	3	4	5
Totally disagree	Disagree	Doesn't apply/ not sure	Agree	Totally agree

5. One or two members dominate the meeting.

1	2	3	4	5
Totally disagree	Disagree	Doesn't apply/ not sure	Agree	Totally agree

Meeting Diagnostic Survey, cont'd

6. Often the meeting ends before everyone has been heard from.

1	2	3	4	5
Totally disagree	Disagree	Doesn't apply/ not sure	Agree	Totally agree

7. People do not address each other directly, but talk about others as if they were not in the room.

1	2	3	4	5
Totally disagree	Disagree	Doesn't apply/ not sure	Agree	Totally agree

8. If the objective of the meeting has not been reached, the group schedules a follow-up meeting rather than run overtime.

1	2	3	4	5
Totally disagree	Disagree	Doesn't apply/ not sure	Agree	Totally agree

9. Many ideas have to be repeated several times before they get a response.

1	2	3	4	5
Totally disagree	Disagree	Doesn't apply/ not sure	Agree	Totally agree

10. The formal leader or chair seems to have more weight than other members.

1	2	3	4	5
Totally disagree	Disagree	Doesn't apply/ not sure	Agree	Totally agree

11. People start to disagree with others before they really understand what's being said.

1	2	3	4	5
Totally disagree	Disagree	Doesn't apply/ not sure	Agree	Totally agree

12. Following meetings, there are postmortems behind closed doors about what really went on.

1	2	3	4	5
Totally disagree	Disagree	Doesn't apply/ not sure	Agree	Totally agree

13. There is never any assessment at the end of meetings to see whether the group has achieved what it set out to do.

1	2	3	4	5
Totally disagree	Disagree	Doesn't apply/ not sure	Agree	Totally agree

Meeting Diagnostic Survey, cont'd

14. People react to new ideas by making fun, uttering put-downs, or ignoring the idea altogether, rather than questioning and exploring it further.

1	2	3	4	5
Totally disagree	Disagree	Doesn't apply/ not sure	Agree	Totally agree

15. Too many people sit in the meetings not really participating.

1	2	3	4	5
Totally disagree	Disagree	Doesn't apply/ not sure	Agree	Totally agree

16. After the meeting, there is always some confusion about what was agreed upon and who is responsible for implementation.

1	2	3	4	5
Totally disagree	Disagree	Doesn't apply/ not sure	Agree	Totally agree

17. Few decisions are made by consensus; the group lets individuals make decisions, or it tends to vote on issues without much preceding discussion/analysis.

1	2	3	4	5
Totally disagree	Disagree	Doesn't apply/ not sure	Agree	Totally agree

18. The group often cannot make decisions because it does not have the necessary information, or people have not done their homework.

1	2	3	4	5
Totally disagree	Disagree	Doesn't apply/ not sure	Agree	Totally agree

19. There is seldom any checking to see whether the group has gone off track, or if the meeting is an effective use of time.

1	2	3	4	5
Totally disagree	Disagree	Doesn't apply/ not sure	Agree	Totally agree

20. Too often we agree on a course of action because everyone is tired, or cannot be bothered to delve deeper.

1	2	3	4	5
Totally disagree	Disagree	Doesn't apply/ not sure	Agree	Totally agree

Meeting Diagnostic Survey, cont'd

21. People seem to leave the meeting drained of energy.

1	2	3	4	5
Totally disagree	Disagree	Doesn't apply/ not sure	Agree	Totally agree

22. The members seem to spend a disproportionate amount of time at the start of meetings trying to define the problem they're supposed to be working on.

1	2	3	4	5
Totally disagree	Disagree	Doesn't apply/ not sure	Agree	Totally agree

23. During meetings people arrive late, ask to be excused early, are frequently called out, and so on.

1	2	3	4	5
Totally disagree	Disagree	Doesn't apply/ not sure	Agree	Totally agree

24. Arguments that have no real bearing on the topic of the meeting often break out.

1	2	3	4	5
Totally disagree	Disagree	Doesn't apply/ not sure	Agree	Totally agree

25. When a serious conflict occurs between some members, no one in the group attempts to help

1	2	3	4	5
Totally disagree	Disagree	Doesn't apply/ not sure	Agree	Totally agree

Additonal Comments:

_____

_____

_____

_____

_____

_____

Our Meetings Are Terrible!

Below are some of the symptoms of dysfunctional meetings and prescriptions for their cure. These are, of course, easier to identify than to fix, but if you can help team members become aware of their patterns, they can begin to resolve them.

SYMPTOMS	CURES
As each person finishes speaking, the next person starts a new topic. There is no building on ideas, thus no continuity of discussion. This results in a half-dozen topics in the air.	Have each person acknowledge the comments of the last speaker. Make it a rule to finish a point before moving forward.
People argue their side, trying to convince others that they're right rather than understanding either the issue or anyone else's input. There is no listening.	Train members to paraphrase what is said in response to their point. Use the flip chart to record all sides of an issue. Get everyone to understand these differing views. Only then, try for a decision.
As soon as a problem is mentioned, someone announces that he or she understands the problem. A solution is very quickly proposed and the discussion moves to another topic.	Use cause and effect diagrams or systematic problem solving to bring structure to meetings. Become thorough in solving problems. Avoid jumping to obvious solutions.
Whenever someone disagrees with a group decision, the dissenting view is ignored.	Develop an ear for dissenting views and make sure they are heard. Have someone else paraphrase the dissenting opinion.
The group uses brainstorming and voting to reach all decisions.	Pre-plan meeting processes so other tools are on hand, and then use them.
Conversations often go nowhere for twenty to thirty minutes. In frustration the group goes on to another topic.	Set a time limit on each discussion and halfway through evaluate how it's going. Use periodic summaries and push for closure.
People often speak in an emotional tone of voice. Sometimes they even say things to others that are quite personal.	Have people stop and rephrase their comments so there are no distracting personal innuendoes.
Group members hold frequent side meetings to discuss what they're thinking. No one says any of this out loud, of course.	Encourage honesty by valuing all input. Draw side chatterers back to the general conversation.
Group members don't notice they've become sidetracked on an issue until they've been off topic for quite awhile.	Call "sidetrack" or have some other signal to flag it. Decide if you want to digress or park the particular issue.
Only the real extroverts, or those with "power," do most of the talking. Some team members say little at most meetings.	Use round robins to get input. Call on members by name. Use idea slips to get written comments from everyone.
No one pays attention to body language or notices that some people have tuned out or even seem agitated.	Make perception checks and ask people to express their feelings.
There is no closure to most topics. Little action takes place between meetings.	Stress closure. Reach a clear decision and record it. Have an action planning form handy. Bring actions forward at the next meeting.
There is little achieved week after week.	Do a meeting evaluation, and discuss the results before the next meeting. Post any new rules or improvement ideas.

The Fundamentals of Meeting Management

1. Create and use a detailed agenda

Each meeting must have an agenda that's been developed ahead of time and ratified by the members of the team. By having the agenda in advance of the meeting, members can do their homework and come prepared to make decisions.

Agendas should include:

__ topics for discussion, plus a brief description of what is involved and what needs to be accomplished

__ a time guideline for each item

__ the name of the person bringing forward the item

__ the details of the process to be used for each discussion

If the agenda cannot be designed in advance for whatever reason, then the first order of business at the meeting must be agenda building. In this facilitated discussion, members design the agenda for that day's session.

2. Develop step-by-step process notes

Most of the books that have been written on meetings do not mention "process notes," largely because these books are geared toward meetings that will be chaired rather than facilitated.

When a meeting is facilitated, there *must* be detailed process notes for each agenda item. These notes specify how the discussion will be facilitated. They specify the tools and techniques to be used, and how participation will be managed.

In the following sample agenda, we've added process notes to illustrate their important role. While some facilitators keep these design notes to themselves, it's often a good idea to enhance buy-in to a process by openly sharing the process with the group (more detailed, process notes can be found in Chapter 9).

Sample agenda with process notes

Name of group: Customer Fulfillment Team
Members: Jane, Muhammed, Jacques, Elaine, Carl, Fred, Diane, Joe
Meeting details: Monday, June 12, 1996, 11:00 to 1:00 (Brown Bag Lunch), Conference Room C

What & Why*	How (process notes)
Warm-up (10 min) – Joe ↪ create focus	• Members share one recent customer contact story
Review agenda and norms (5 min) — Joe ↪ To set context	• Ratify the agenda and the norms through general discussion. Add any new items — make sure there is clarity about the overall goal of the meeting
Bring forward action items (25 min) — all ↪ Implementation monitoring	• Brief report back by all members on action plans created at the last meeting — addition of any new plans

What & Why*	How (process notes)
Focus group updates (20 min) — Jacques & Diane → To identify areas for improvement	• Report on the outcomes of six customer focus groups. Use force-field analysis to distinguish between what we are doing well and what we aren't
Prioritization of customer issues (20 min) — Joe → To set priorities	• Establish criteria to evaluate customer concerns • Use criteria matrix to appraise each issue and determine top priorities for action
Problem solving of priority issues (30 min) — entire group → To create improvement plans	• Divide into two sub-teams to problem solve the two top-priority issues; create detailed action plans for the top issues; meet as a group to share and ratify ideas
Next-step planning & agenda building (10 min) — Joe → To ensure closure & design next session	• Make sure people know what they're expected to work on; start to form agenda for the next meeting
Exit survey (10 min) — Joe → To check meeting effectiveness	• Have people evaluate the meeting on their way out the door • Identify items to be brought forward at the next meeting

Note: *Times given above are totally speculative and are only included for illustration purposes.*

3. Clarify roles and responsibilities
Effective meetings require people to play defined roles.

Facilitator: designs the methodology for the meeting, manages participation, offers useful tools, helps the group determine its needs, keeps things on track and periodically checks on how things are going. A facilitator doesn't influence *what* is being discussed, but instead focuses on *how* issues are being discussed. A facilitator is a procedural expert who is there to help and support the group's effectiveness. Facilitation is focused on asking.

Chairperson: runs the meeting according to defined rules, but also offers opinions and engages in the discussion if he or she chooses. The chairperson has traditionally not been neutral. Most often, the chairperson of any meeting is the official leader, who plays an active role as decision maker and "opinion leader."

Minute taker: takes brief, accurate notes of what's discussed and the decisions made. Also responsible for incorporating the notes on flip charts. Most often, minute-taking responsibilities are rotated among the regular members of a work group. However, for special meetings or if money isn't a barrier, this role can be played by someone not involved in the discussion.

Timekeeper: a rotating role in which someone keeps track of the time and reminds the group periodically if they're staying within guidelines. Not a license to be autocratic or shut down important discussions if they're running over. The use of an automatic timer will let the timekeeper participate in the discussion more comfortably.

Scribe: a group member who volunteers to write/record comments on a flip chart. Some facilitators are more comfortable asking others to make notes on the flip chart while they facilitate. This has the benefit of freeing the facilitator from the distractions of writing, but adds its own complications. The scribe may start facilitating or may not make the notes the way the facilitator wants. Having a scribe takes a lot of coordination. Since a scribe takes a second person out of the discussion, a general rule is that a facilitator should make his or her own notes if at all possible. If a scribe is used, clarifying questions should be channeled through the facilitator, instead of the scribe interacting directly with the members.

Balancing the Roles of Chairperson and Facilitator

Chairing and facilitating are two distinct meeting management styles. Each has its strengths and its place.

Chairing is most useful at the start of a meeting in order to go over minutes, share information and manage a round-robin report-back by members. Chairing traditionally relies on the use of "Parliamentary Rules of Order."

Since chairs are not neutral, their major drawback is that they tend to influence decisions and concentrate power. It's not uncommon for a strong chairperson to make final decisions on important items.

A consequence of this decision mode is that the chair "owns" the outcome. There is also little emphasis of using process tools when playing the traditional role of the chairperson.

Facilitating is designed to foster the full and equal participation of all members when their input is needed to decide issues. Because facilitators are neutral, they empower members. They rely on consensus and collaboration to reach important decisions. This results in decisions for which the whole group feels it has ownership.

Facilitation creates rules from within the group, rather than imposing rules from a book. Facilitation is also associated with a rich array of tools and techniques designed to create synergy and get better ideas.

A very common role arrangement is to have a meeting leader who uses a chairperson approach to start the meeting and deal with the agenda, and take care of the housekeeping and information-sharing portions of the session, and then switch to facilitation in order to get input on specific topics within the agenda.

When chairing, you need to know when to switch hats and become facilitative.

All good facilitators should know when and how to act as an effective chairperson. Conversely, it would be ideal if all chairpersons were also skilled facilitators, who could switch styles when they wanted to get participation and ownership.

With some planning beforehand, these roles don't need to conflict. The key is to remember that each has its place, and to be clear about which approach is being used.

In summary:

Chair when you want to	Facilitate when you want to
• review past minutes and agenda items	• increase participation
• exchange information	• shift ownership
• hear members report back	• get members to make decisions
• discuss next steps	• get members to create action plans

4. Set clear meeting norms

Make sure that the group has clear norms for behavior and that those norms are created by the group. Help the group tailor its norms to meet the demands of particular meetings by helping members set targeted norms if applicable. (Refer to Targeted Norms, page 74.)

5. Manage participation

Make sure that everyone is part of the discussion, that structure exists for each item, and that there is effective use of decision-making tools to bring closure to all items.

As facilitator, you are responsible for ensuring that members know and exhibit effective discussion skills. If members are not skilled, then you should conduct the training exercises suggested on page 79 or use other strategies discussed in Chapter 4.

6. Make periodic process checks

Process checking is a technique that every facilitator should utilize during meetings to keep meetings from going "off the rails." It involves stopping the discussion and turning the group's attention to how the meeting is going. The purpose of this shift in focus is to engage members in checking how things are being done and what changes are needed to improve the flow of the meeting.

There are basically four elements in process checking:

1. Check for progress: Ask members whether they think the goals are being achieved. Are problems being solved? Are decisions being made?

When to check progress: If things seem to be getting stuck; at points of closure; at least once per session.

2. *Check the pace:* Ask whether things are moving too quickly or too slowly. Get any suggestions for improving the pace, and implement these immediately.

When to check the pace: When things seem to be dragging or moving too fast; any time people look frustrated; at least once per session/meeting.

3. *Check the process:* Ask members if the tool or approach being used is working or needs to be changed. Ask for or offer suggestions for another approach.

When to check the process: When the tool isn't yielding the results you hoped for, or it's evident that the process isn't being followed as laid out.

4. *Take the pulse:* Ask members how they're feeling: are they energized? Tired? Do they feel satisfied or frustrated? Ask for their suggestions on how to perk things up.

When to take the pulse: Any time members look distracted, tired or frustrated; at least once during each session.

How to Do a Process Check

Process checks can be done verbally by asking members directly, or in written form by posting the survey below on a flip chart near the door. Members can then anonymously rate how the meeting is going thus far. When members return from the break, ask them to interpret the survey results and brainstorm ideas for improving the remainder of the session. Act on their suggestions immediately.

 ## Sample Process Check Survey

Tell us how it's going so far.

Progress: *To what extent are we achieving our goals?*

1	2	3	4	5
Poor	Fair	Satisfactory	Good	Excellent

Pace: *How does the pace feel?*

1	2	3	4	5
Far too slow	Slow	Just right	Fast	Far too fast

Process: *Are we using the right methods/tools?*

1	2	3	4	5
Not at all		Somewhat		Extremely effective

Pulse: *How are you feeling about the session? Put a check mark beside any that describe you now.*

1	2	3	4	5
Totally frustrated	Exhausted	Satisfied	Pleased	Energized

7. Take minutes

Assign responsibility for taking very brief, concise notes to someone in the group. Because people are so swamped with paper and e-mails these days, the best minutes are short one-page summaries of what was decided and next steps.

8. Determine next steps

Never let a group leave a meeting without clear next steps in place. This means defining what will be done, by whom and when. These action plans need to be brought forward at all subsequent meetings to make sure that the group is following through on commitments.

9. Evaluate the meeting

Always get the group to review and evaluate each meeting. This evaluation should include what can be done to improve the next meeting and some feedback for the facilitator.

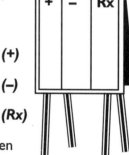

There are three ways to evaluate a meeting:

1. Force-Field Analysis — this involves asking
"What were the strengths of today's meeting?" **(+)**

"What were the weaknesses?" **(–)**

"What should we do to correct the weaknesses?" **(Rx)**

2. Exit Survey — three to six questions are written on a sheet of flip chart paper, and posted near an exit. Members fill it out upon leaving the meeting. The results are then discussed at the start of the next meeting. On the next page you'll find a sample Meeting Exit Survey that may be useful.

3. Formal Survey — hand the survey out to members to complete. After being tabulated, the results are discussed at a subsequent meeting. This is an appropriate exercise to be done three or four times a year for any ongoing group or team. A sample formal Meeting Effectiveness Survey is provided on page 146. The Survey Feedback process is described on page 193 in Chapter 9 of this book.

Sample Meeting Exit Survey

Give us your assessment of the items below.

Output — How well did we achieve what we needed to?

1	2	3	4	5
Poor	Fair	Satisfactory	Good	Excellent

Use of time — How well did we use our time?

1	2	3	4	5
Poor	Fair	Satisfactory	Good	Excellent

Participation — How well did we do on making sure everyone was involved equally?

1	2	3	4	5
Poor	Fair	Satisfactory	Good	Excellent

Decision Making — How well-thought-out were our decisions?

1	2	3	4	5
Poor	Fair	Satisfactory	Good	Excellent

Action Plans — How clear and doable are our action plans?

1	2	3	4	5
Poor	Fair	Satisfactory	Good	Excellent

Organization — How well was the meeting run?

1	2	3	4	5
Poor	Fair	Satisfactory	Good	Excellent

Meeting Effectiveness Survey

Instructions: Please give your candid opinions of the meetings you attended as part of this group. Rate the characteristics of the meetings by circling the appropriate number on each scale to represent your evaluation. Remain anonymous. Return the survey to your group facilitator. *Remember, you are rating the meetings of this group.*

1. MEETING OBJECTIVES
Are objectives clearly set out in advance of the meeting?

| 1 | 2 | 3 | 4 | 5 | 6 | 7 |

Objectives are seldom set out in advance   Objectives are always set out in advance

2. COMMUNICATION
Are agendas circulated to all members in advance of the meeting?

| 1 | 2 | 3 | 4 | 5 | 6 | 7 |

Agendas are rarely circulated in advance   Agendas are always circulated in advance

3. START TIMES
Do meetings start on time?

| 1 | 2 | 3 | 4 | 5 | 6 | 7 |

Meetings hardly ever start on time   Meetings always start on time

4. TIME LIMITS
Are time limits set for each agenda item?

| 1 | 2 | 3 | 4 | 5 | 6 | 7 |

We do not set time limits   Time limits are always set for each item

5. MEETING REVIEW
Are action items from the previous meeting(s) brought forward?

| 1 | 2 | 3 | 4 | 5 | 6 | 7 |

Items are seldom brought forward   Items are always brought forward from previous meetings

6. WARM-UP
Is there a meeting warm-up to hear from all members?

| 1 | 2 | 3 | 4 | 5 | 6 | 7 |

We seldom use a meeting warm-up   We often use a meeting warm-up

Meeting Effectiveness Survey, cont'd

7. ROLE CLARITY

Are roles (i.e. timekeeper, scribe, facilitator) made clear?

1	2	3	4	5	6	7

Roles are not identified   Roles are always clearly defined

8. SETTING

Is there a quiet place for the meeting, with ample work space, flip charts and AV support?

1	2	3	4	5	6	7

The meeting place is not well suited   The meeting place is very good

9. PROCESS

Is there clarity before each topic as to how that item will be managed?

1	2	3	4	5	6	7

There is rarely any planning on process   There is always clarity on process

10. PREPARATION

Does everyone come prepared and ready to make decisions?

1	2	3	4	5	6	7

We are often unprepared   We are generally prepared

11. INTERRUPTIONS

Are meetings being disrupted due to people leaving, phones ringing, pagers beeping, etc.

1	2	3	4	5	6	7

There are constant interruptions   We control interruptions

12. PARTICIPATION

Are all members fully exchanging views, taking responsibility for action items and follow-up?

1	2	3	4	5	6	7

People hold back and don't take ownership   Everyone offers ideas and takes action

13. LEADERSHIP

Does one person make all the decisions, or is there a sharing of authority?

1	2	3	4	5	6	7

The manager holds the chair and makes most decisions   Authority is shared

14. PACE

How would you rate the pace of the meetings?

1	2	3	4	5	6	7

Poor   Just right

15. TRACKING

Do meetings stay on track and follow the agenda?

1	2	3	4	5	6	7

Meetings ususally stray   Meetings usually
off track   stay on track

16. RECORD KEEPING

Are quality minutes kept and circulated?

1	2	3	4	5	6	7

Yes, they are   No, they are not

17. LISTENING

Do members practice active listening?

1	2	3	4	5	6	7

We don't listen closely   Members listen
to each other   actively

18. CONFLICT MANAGEMENT

Are differences of opinion suppressed, or is conflict effectively used?

1	2	3	4	5	6	7

Conflict isn't very   Conflict is effectively
effectively used   exploited for new ideas

19. DECISION MAKING

Does the group generally make good decisions at our meetings?

1	2	3	4	5	6	7

We tend to make   We tend to make
poor decisions   good decisions

20. CLOSURE

Do we tend to end topics before getting into new ones?

1	2	3	4	5	6	7

We constantly start   We close each topic
new topics   before moving on

Meeting Effectiveness Survey, cont'd

21. CONSENSUS

Do we work hard to make collaborative decisions that we can all live with?

1	2	3	4	5	6	7

We abandon consensus too easily   We work hard to reach consensus

22. FOLLOW-UP

Is there good coherent follow-up to commitments made at meetings?

1	2	3	4	5	6	7

We tend not to follow up   There is consistent follow-up

✏️ *Notes*

_____

_____

_____

_____

_____

_____

_____

_____

_____

_____

_____

_____

_____

_____

_____

_____

_____

_____

_____

_____

_____

_____

_____

Chapter 8
Process Tools for Facilitators

*I*magine a carpenter trying to build a house without the proper tools. It would certainly be ineffective if not altogether impossible! Regardless of the job, you need the right tools. Fortunately for facilitators, there is a rich set of tools available.

Since dozens of tools exist, it would be impossible to explain them all. Only the most often used tools will be highlighted in this chapter. This set represents the basic processes that every facilitator must know how and when to use.

You'll find a detailed description of each on the following pages.

- **Visioning**
- **Brainstorming**
- **Gap Analysis**
- **Decision Grids**
- **Priority Setting**
- **Systematic Problem Solving**
- **Survey Feedback**

- **Sequential Questioning**
- **Force-Field Analysis**
- **Multi-voting**
- **Troubleshooting**
- **Needs and Offers Negotiation**
- **Root-Cause Analysis**

Know how and when to use the core process tools

In addition to these tools, all facilitators should learn the techniques associated with quality improvement such as process mapping, mind mapping, affinity diagrams, pareto analysis, tree diagrams, sequence flow charting, control charts, storyboarding, SWAT analysis, histograms, scatter diagrams, flow charts and critical path charts.

Visioning

What is it? A highly participative approach to goal setting for groups of anywhere from six to more than 100 members.

When should you use it? When members need to clarify their own thoughts and then share those ideas with each other to create a clear shared statement of the desired future.

What is its purpose? Allows people to put forward their ideas. Makes sure everyone is involved and heard from. Creates energy. Gets people aligned. Gives people a creative method to identify a group goal.

What's the outcome? This visioning process is very participative and energizes everyone in the room. It also creates buy-in because the group's direction is coming from the members themselves. Everyone is involved at once. All ideas are heard. This is a great way to conduct goal setting with a group.

How Does Visioning Work?

Step #1. Post a series of questions that relate to the task and ask how the final outcome ought to look at a future point in time. The vision questions will always be different, of course, depending on the situation.

> ### Sample Visioning Questions for a Customer Service Improvement Team
> Imagine that it's exactly two years from today:
> - *Describe how you now serve customers.*
> - *What specific improvements have been made?*
> - *What are people saying about the team now?*
> - *What problems has the group solved?*
> - *What specific outcomes have been achieved?*
> - *How are people behaving differently?*

Step #2: Ask each person to write down his or her own responses to the questions. Allow at least five minutes. Give more time if needed. Ask people not to speak to each other during this writing phase.

Step #3: Ask everyone to get a partner. Allocate three to five minutes for the first partner to share his or her vision. Ask the other partner to facilitate. After three to five minutes, ask the partners to switch roles so that the second person gets to talk.

Step #4: When time is up, ask everyone to find another partner. Repeat the process outlined in step 3, only allow slightly less time per person. Encourage people to "steal" any good ideas they got from their last partner and incorporate these into their own vision.

Step #5: Repeat the process again with new partners. This time, limit the exchange to one to three minutes per person in order to force people to prioritize and share the highlights.

☑ Tip: You can keep switching partners until everyone has spoken to everyone else. This creates lots of energy!

Step #6: Ask people to return to their original seats, and then begin facilitating a discussion to pull the ideas together. You'll find that ideas have become fairly homogenized by this point.

☑ Tip: A good way to proceed is question by question, and have everyone just read all ideas on that item. Then, ask people what themes they heard repeated, and record these.

Sequential Questioning

What is it? An assessment exercise conducted in the form of a series of questions. These are posed to the whole group at the start of a workshop.

When should you use it? To uncover important information about the group, their issues or activities. To test and probe in a challenging manner. To raise issues, and create discontent with the status quo.

What is its purpose? Yields information, lets you test assumptions and challenge people. Gets people to surface their negativity and cynicism. Vents negative feelings and creates an obvious need to take action. Helps the facilitator anticipate the issues that might come up throughout the day. When done well, this technique creates a shared desire to make change happen. It certainly warms up the group.

What is the outcome? Sequential questioning is a challenging technique that creates sparks. It raises issues and gets people talking about the barriers. It raises people's consciousness about what the important problems are. It sets the stage for problem solving and solution development.

Since there is potential for disagreement, if you plan to use sequential questioning, you have to be prepared to make interventions and manage any conflicts that arise.

How Does Sequential Questioning Work?

Step #1: Analyze the overall topic and create about ten questions working from macro to micro issues. Each question should probe the situation in a challenging way so that the ensuing discussion reveals honest information important to the issue at hand.

Step #2: Write only one question at the top of each sheet of flip chart paper. Use the rest of the sheet to record reactions. Don't let people see the questions until you pose them. As you turn over each sheet, ask only one person in the group to respond. Record that person's response. Then, invite others to add their thoughts.

☑Tip: Build questions around issues people identified in pre-workshop interviews. Pose the questions as closed-ended questions or items to be rated on a scale. Choose someone to answer yes or no, to each item. Then ask others whether they agree or disagree. Discuss people's reasons for their answers until you and the group can formulate a summary statement about how everyone feels about each question.

While sample questions are offered on the next page, remember that these questions always need to be created to fit each particular situation.

Sample Sequential Questions

<u>Workshop:</u> *Focus on Business Improvement*

Answer **yes** or **no,** then explain your response.

yes or **no** Rationale➤	The overall business environment for the next five years is going to be advantageous for our business.
yes or **no** Rationale➤	We are fully prepared to handle all the opportunities that will occur in the next five years.
yes or **no** Rationale➤	Our current business development strategy is dynamic and flexible enough to respond to constant changes in the business environment.
yes or **no** Rationale➤	Our business strategy should be developed by people at the higher levels.
yes or **no** Rationale➤	Our staff are ready and motivated to overcome barriers.
yes or **no** Rationale➤	We really understand our customers' needs and wants.
yes or **no** Rationale➤	We have an early warning and performance measurement system that lets us track our progress and make timely corrections.
yes or **no** Rationale➤	There is a high level of harmony and cooperation that ensures synergy and teamwork inside our organization.
yes or **no** Rationale➤	We have the best products on the market. We own the market in our field.
yes or **no** Rationale➤	We have a fairly flawless delivery system for getting our product to our customers.
yes or **no** Rationale➤	We often have creative business development discussions during our regular meetings. Better customer service is a topic we discuss all the time.

Brainstorming

What is it? A technique for getting bigger and better ideas. Puts a full range of ideas on the table before decisions are made.

When should you use it? To generate a free flow of creative ideas that are not bound by the usual barriers. To get everyone involved. To create energy. To generate a wide range of solutions for a problem.

What is its purpose? Allows people to explore new ideas and challenge traditional thinking. Lets people put ideas on the table without fear of being corrected or challenged. It separates the creation of ideas from the evaluation activity.

What is the outcome? A long list of creative ideas from which to work. Since brainstorming frees people from practical considerations, it encourages them to think creatively. It's also an energizing process that helps move people to take action. Because it's highly participative, brainstorming makes everyone feel that they're an important part of the solution.

How Does Brainstorming Work?

Step #1: Announce that you will be using brainstorming. Review the rules:
- Let ideas flow freely
- No evaluating of ideas until later
- Build on the ideas of others
- Be humorous and creative
- There are no bad ideas
- No debating
- Everyone participates
- Think in new ways; break out of old patterns
- Keep discussion moving

Step #2: Clarify the topic being brainstormed, then allow a few minutes of quiet while people think about solutions.

Step #3: Ask members to let their ideas flow. The actual brainstorming can be structured (go systematically around the group), or be spontaneous (members offer ideas as they come to mind).

Step #4: Record ideas as they're generated. Do not discuss or elaborate on them. Keep it moving.

Step #5: When people have run out of ideas, allow for a few minutes of thinking time and reflection. Sometimes the best ideas emerge in the second round.

Step #6: When there really are no further suggestions, discuss each brainstormed idea in detail so that it's fully developed and clearly understood. Combine similar ideas that are simply worded differently.

Step #7: Use a decision grid (page 161) or multi-voting (page 159) to sort the good ideas from the poor ones.

Step #8: Agree on the final list of best ideas.

Anonymous Brainstorming Technique

What is it? An idea generation technique that asks people to write down their ideas, then pass them to other group members who build on them.

When should you use it? When people are reluctant to speak in front of others, or when there are outspoken members who would dominate a verbal brainstorming session. Also useful if the issue or topic is sensitive, since the initial idea generation step is anonymous and private.

What is its purpose? The anonymity of this tool gives people the freedom to express their ideas.

What's the outcome? Idea building generates lots of ideas. It also allows people to build on each other's ideas in an anonymous setting.

How Does Anonymous Brainstorming Work?

Step #1: Clarify the topic or issue for which ideas will be generated. Explain the process to members.

Step #2: Give each person small slips of paper. Ask members to work alone as they think of ideas to resolve the issue being discussed. Allow anywhere from three to 10 minutes for the idea generation step.

Step #3: Ask members to fold their idea sheets and toss them into the center of the table. (Slips should not have names on them.)

Step #4: Mix the sheets and ask each person to take back as many as he or she tossed in. If anyone pulls out his/her own slip, that person can toss it back, or exchange it with a neighbor.

Step #5: Each person now has five to 10 minutes to add his or her thoughts to build on the original idea on each sheet picked from the pile. The slips can then be passed to a third person to generate further ideas.

Step #6: Once all ideas have been developed, ask all members to read their suggestions out loud.

Step #7: Discuss ideas and record them on the flip chart.

Step #8: Use a decision grid (page 161) or multi-voting (page 159) to find the best ideas to fit the situation.

Force-Field Analysis

What is it? Force-field analysis is a structured method of looking at the two opposing forces acting on a situation.

When should you use it? When you need to surface all of the factors at play in a situation, so that barriers and problems can be identified.

What is its purpose? Clarifies the resources available, and also the barriers or obstacles. Helps groups understand what they need to do to succeed.

What is the outcome? Force-field analysis is a valuable tool for analyzing situations and identifying problems that need to be solved. It helps groups make more effective decisions because it lets members look at both positive and negative forces at play.

How Does Force-Field Analysis Work?

Step #1: Identify a topic, situation or project, such as, say, computer training.

Step #2: Help the group state the goal. Example: *"All staff will receive training in the new operating system in three weeks."*

Step #3: Draw a line down the center of a flip chart sheet. Use one side to identify all of the forces (resources, skills, attitudes) that will help reach the goal. On the other side, identify all the forces that could hinder reaching the goal (barriers, problems, deficiencies, etc.)

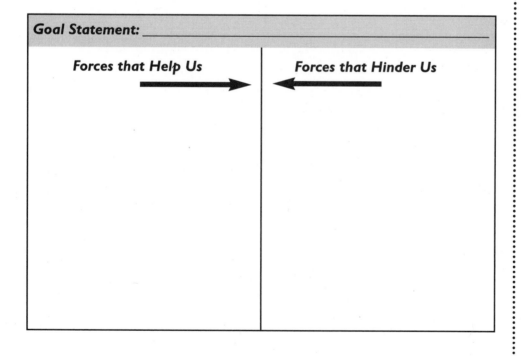

Goal Statement: _____

Forces that Help Us	**Forces that Hinder Us**

Step #4: Once all help and hinder items have been identified, use a decision grid or multi-voting (see this chapter) to determine which of the hindrances or barriers are a priority for immediate problem solving.

Step #5: Address the priority barriers using the *Systematic Problem-Solving Model* (see page 170).

Variations of Force-Field Analysis

Force-field analysis has a number of variations. Each one has been created using roughly the same steps as described previously.

These variations include:

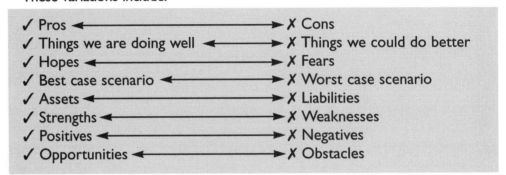

✓ Pros ←→ ✗ Cons
✓ Things we are doing well ←→ ✗ Things we could do better
✓ Hopes ←→ ✗ Fears
✓ Best case scenario ←→ ✗ Worst case scenario
✓ Assets ←→ ✗ Liabilities
✓ Strengths ←→ ✗ Weaknesses
✓ Positives ←→ ✗ Negatives
✓ Opportunities ←→ ✗ Obstacles

Gap Analysis

What is it? A means of identifying blocks to achieving a desired goal.

When should you use it? When a group needs to understand the gap between where they currently are and where they ultimately want to end up.

What is its purpose? Gap analysis lets you explore the missing steps between where you are and where you want to go. It forces a realistic look at the present and helps identify the things that need to be done to arrive at the desired future.

What is the outcome? Gap analysis is a planning tool that creates alignment between group members as to what needs to be done to eliminate the gap between where they currently are (present state) and where they ideally would like to be (desired future state).

How Does Gap Analysis Work?

Step #1: Identify the future state. Use visioning or any other approach that yields a picture of where the group wants to be at a specific time. The description of the future must be detailed. Post the information on the right-hand side of a large work space on a wall.

Step #2: Identify the present state. How are things now? Describe the same components featured in the future state, only do so in real, present terms. Again be very detailed. Post the ideas generated on the left-hand side of the wall work space.

Step #3: Focus on the gaps. Ask members to work with a partner to discuss:

- *What are the gaps?*
- *What are the other barriers?*
- *What's missing?*

Step #4: Share ideas as a group and post these on the wall between the "present" and the "future."

Step #5: Once there is consensus on the gaps, divide the large group into subgroups and give each group one or more gap items to problem solve.

Step #6: Reassemble the whole group to hear recommendations and action plans.

Step #7: Ratify the plans by getting acceptance from all other members; then create a mechanism for follow-up.

PRESENT STATE	GAP	DESIRED FUTURE
Teams operate without leaders for months because there aren't enough people trained	No team-leader training program	A trained cadre of team leaders

Multi-Voting

What is it? A decision-making tool that enables a group to sort through a long list of ideas to identify priorities.

When should you use it? When a group has to discuss a long list of items, and then has to quickly identify which one(s) should be dealt with immediately.

What is its purpose? Quickly establishes a clear set of priorities.

What is the outcome? Multi-voting is democratic and participative. Since most members will see at least one or more of the items that they voted for near the top of the priority list, this form of voting does not create the sense of winners and losers that majority voting does.

How Does Multi-Voting Work?

Step #1: Clarify the items being prioritized. This may be a list of barriers from a force-field analysis, or a list of ideas from a brainstorming exercise. Have members discuss each item, what it means, its strengths and weaknesses, and so on, to make sure people understand the choices they're making.

Step #2: Identify criteria to guide the vote more specifically so that people don't vote at cross-purposes. Make sure that everyone votes with the same criteria in mind. The *criteria* could be one or more of the following:

- the lowest cost items
- the easiest items to complete
- the first items in a logical sequence
- the most important items
- the most innovative items
- the most important to the customer

Step #3: Once the criteria are clear, there are two methods for conducting a multi-vote.

Method 1: Voting with sticker dots

- Using colored, peel-off file-folder dots, hand out a strip of four to seven dots to each person. Use slightly fewer dots than half the items to be sorted to force people to make choices (i.e. give out four dots to sort 10 items).
- Ask members to put four stickers on their top four choices listed on the flip chart. (Ensure that no one puts all four stickers on one choice.)
- When everyone has voted, tally the dots in order to arrive at the priorities.

Method 2: Distributing points

- Give each person points (usually 10 or 100) to distribute among the items to be sorted.
- Members then place their points beside the items they favor. It's wise not to allow anyone to place more than 50 percent of their points on any single item.
- When everyone has voted, add the scores to arrive at the priorities.

Root-Cause Analysis

What is it? A systematic analysis of an issue to identify the root causes rather than the symptoms.

When should you use it? When you need to delve beyond surface symptoms and uncover the underlying causes of problems.

What is its purpose? Leads to more complete and final solutions.

What is the outcome? Root-cause analysis forces groups to look more deeply at problems and to deal with the underlying causes. This often means that problems are more likely to be resolved once and for all.

How Does Root-Cause Analysis Work?

Step #1: Explain the difference between "causes" and their "effects" to group members. For example, you can ask whether a noisy muffler is a cause or an effect. Once people have identified that it's an effect, ask them to list all of the causes. Point out that effects can't be solved, but underlying causes can.

Step #2: You now have a choice of two basic methods, as described below, for determining root cause(s): *Cause & Effect Charting or Fishbone Diagrams.*

Step #3: Once all causes are identified, brainstorm solutions for each one.

Method #1: Cause and Effect Charting

i) When analyzing a problem, divide a flip chart sheet in two, and write effects on the right side and causes on the left. Example: Noisy Muffler.

Cause	*Effect*
• corrosion	• noise and fumes
• loose clamps	when accelerating
• puncture	

ii) Whenever anyone offers a point of analysis ask whether it's a cause or effect. Write each item in its appropriate column. Probe each item in the effect column to determine what causes it. Continue until all causes have been identified.

Method # 2: Fishbone Diagrams

Use a fishbone diagram to sort all of the contributing causes for the problem being analyzed systematically. The cause categories on fishbone charts vary, but usually include people, machinery/equipment, methods, materials, policies, environment and measurement. The number of categories will vary.

i) Start by placing the observed effect at the "head" of the fishbone. Determine the major cause categories, then ask members to brainstorm all of the possible causes on each "rib" of the fish. For example:

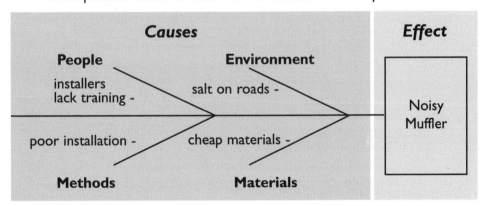

ii) Once all of the causes have been identified, ask the group to brainstorm solutions for each of them, or use multi-voting to sort which causes are their highest priority for being solved.

Decision Grid

What is it? A matrix of critical criteria used to assess a set of ideas, in order to determine which one(s) are most likely to offer the best solution(s).

When should you use it? When you need to bring more objectivity and thoroughness to the decision-making process.

What is its purpose? Changes the decision-making process from one in which members debate which solutions they feel are most suitable, to one in which each potential solution is objectively judged against the same set of criteria.

What is the outcome? Clear, sorted ideas emerge from a mass of random brainstormed thoughts. Grids also make the sorting process more systematic. Since everyone gets to cast votes or express opinions, the use of grids is participative and democratic.

How Does the Decision Grid Work?

Once members have brainstormed a set of ideas to solve a problem, create a decision grid. Two types of decision grids are illustrated: *criteria-based* or *impact-effort based.*

A. Criteria-Based Grids

Step #1: Ask members to identify the criteria against which all of the potential solutions willl be judged. Examples are:

- saves time
- saves money
- reduces stress
- is timely
- is doable
- is affordable
- is fast
- supports the strategic plan
- is something we can control
- represents the right sequence
- builds empowerment
- will get management support
- satisfies customer needs
- doesn't disrupt our operation

Step #2: The top three to five criteria are chosen from this list and placed along the top of a grid. The options being considered are placed down the left column.

Step #3: Each option is then evaluated as to the extent to which it meets each criteria that the group has selected. Note that some criteria may be more important than others, and hence given more weight.

Rate each solution against the criteria as follows:

1 = does not meet the criteria
2 = somewhat meets the criteria
3 = good at meeting the criteria

Step #4: Add up the scores to determine which solutions will be implemented.

Decision Grid Example:
Decision grid for assessing solutions to the challenge of getting 50 people training in new software in 14 days.

		Criteria				
		Cost Effective (x 1)	**Meets Customer Needs** (x 3)**	**Speed (x 1)**	**Lack of Disruption (x 1)**	**Totals per Solution**
Possible Solutions	Shut down to give each person two days' classroom training	1 2 1 1 ÷ 4 = 1.25	1 1 1 1 ÷ 4= 1.00	3 3 3 3 ÷ 4 = 3.00	1 1 1 1 ÷ 4 = 1.00	**8.25**
	Have 10 experts on site for two weeks to give one-to-one support	2 2 2 1 ÷ 4 = 1.75	2 3 2 2 ÷ 4 = 2.25	1 2 1 1 ÷ 4 = 1.25	3 3 3 3 ÷ 4 = 3.00	**12.75**
	Have 10 people off at training each two-day period	2 2 3 3 ÷ 4 = 2.50	2 3 3 2 ÷ 4 = 2.50	2 2 2 2 ÷ 4 = 2.00	2 2 2 3 ÷ 4 = 2.25	**14.25**

**Four individuals have rated here. The average was calculated by dividing the sum total of the ratings by the number of individuals participating (1 2 1 1 ÷ 4 = 1.25).*

***If any of the criteria is more important than the others, it can be given a multiplier factor (ie: x3). In the above example "meet(s) customers needs" is three times more important than the other criteria.*

Step #4: Create action plans for top-ranked items.

B. Impact/Effort Grids

Step #1: Post all ideas on a nearby wall and draw the impact/effort grid on a sheet of flip chart paper.

		– *Effort* –	
		Difficult to Do	Easy to Do
– *Impact* –	Major Improvement	**3.**	**1.**
	Minor Improvement	**4.**	**2.**

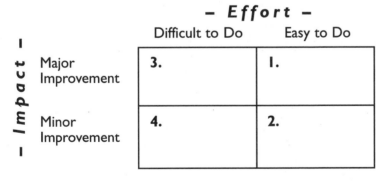

Step #2: Discuss the brainstormed ideas one by one and place each in one of the four boxes. All items are eventually classified as being:

1. Easy to do and yields a big improvement
2. Easy to do but yields a small improvement
3. Difficult to do but yields a big improvement
4. Difficult to do and yields small improvement

Category 1 items are implemented immediately

Category 2 items are also implemented immediately

Category 3 items are the subject of detailed action planning

Category 4 items are discarded

The major difficulty in using an impact/effort grid lies in clarifying exactly what is meant by "easy to do," "difficult to do," "small improvement" and "big improvement," because everyone will understand these terms differently. Being clear at the start will avoid a lot of heated debate later.

<u>**Special Note**</u>: *Impact/effort grids are easier to use than criteria grids because there is no need to create criteria and the grid has already been designed.*

Troubleshooting

What is it? A process for identifying potential problems and creating plans to overcome them.

When should you use it? When it's important to identify barriers to success and create action plans to deal with them.

What is its purpose? Helps a group make sure its action plans are realistic and well thought out.

What is the outcome? Groups gain more control over their activities in spite of a constantly changing and challenging workplace. They're also less likely to be "surprised" by circumstances.

How Does Troubleshooting Work?

Step #1: After a group has created action plans, ask members to consider a series of questions. These questions force a critical look at the circumstances that might impede the activity. For example:

What are the difficult, complex or sensitive aspects of our action plan?
What shifts in the environment, like a change of priorities, should we keep our eye on?
What organizational blocks or barriers could we run into?
What technical or materials-related problems could stop or delay us?
What human resource issues should we be aware of at this point?
In which ways might members of this team not fulfill their commitments?

Step #2: Once potential barriers have been identified, ask members to identify strategies and action plans to overcome each one.

Step #3: Have the group write up its troubleshooting plans in detail. Identify who will monitor follow-through. The following worksheet should help you lead the discussion.

Troubleshooting Worksheet

Activity Being Planned:_____

What could go wrong, block us or change suddenly?	What actions do we need to take to overcome each block? (what, how, by whom, when)

When will we follow up on our planned action steps?

_____
_____
_____
_____
_____

Who's responsible for monitoring this plan?

_____
_____
_____
_____
_____

Survey Feedback

What is it? A group process that involves gathering information and feeding it back to the members so that they can interpret the data and take actions they feel are appropriate.

When should you use it? When there is a problem that group members need to address, about which they lack information.

What is its purpose? It gives the group a means of assessing how it's doing and provides a method for creating actions to resolve any identified problems.

What is the outcome? Members (not the team leader or facilitator) interpret the survey results. This builds commitment and accountability. Members face their problems and deal with them in a productive manner.

How Does It Work?

Step #1: Design and conduct an anonymous survey. This can be about:
- how meetings are run
- the effectiveness of the group
- the performance of the group leader
- the effectiveness of a process
- the satisfaction of customers

Step #2: After the surveys have been filled out, they are returned to a designated member of the group. This person tabulates the survey results by combining all of the responses onto one survey form. The person doing the tabulation doesn't interpret the results; he or she just accurately combines the ratings from the individual surveys.

Step #3: Share the tabulated survey results with the group at a meeting. After members have had an opportunity to read the results, ask them two questions:

1. What is the survey data telling us is going well? Which items got high ratings?

2. What is the survey data telling us is a problem or issue? Which items got low ratings?*

(* A rating is generally considered low if the ratings from "satisfactory" downward are greater than the ratings for items four and five combined. In some cases (i.e. small groups) even one poor rating will indicate that the item needs attention.)

In the example below, nine out of 14 ratings were scored equal to or below *satisfactory,* which means that this item is a cause for concern.

poor		satisfactory		excellent
1	2	3	4	5
✖✖	✖✖✖	✖✖✖✖	✖✖✖	✖✖

Step #4: Once members have identified all of the items that received low enough ratings to be of concern, have them rank these in terms of priority to determine which should be dealt with right away.

Since not every issue can be problem solved, use multi-voting to determine this priority. Ask members:

> *"If we could only solve four of the problems identified, which four should we tackle first?"*

Step #5: Once the top priorities are clear, divide the members into subgroups of no fewer than four individuals. Give each subgroup one issue to work on for about 20 minutes. Deal with as many issues as group size allows.

In subgroups, members will answer two sets of questions about the item they have been given:

- *Why did this item get a low rating? What's wrong here? What is the nature of the problem?* (group members analyze the problem)
- *What are possible solutions for this problem? What will remedy the situation?* (they generate solutions)

Step #6: Reassemble members and have them share their recommendations. Encourage other members to comment and add their ideas. Select the best ideas and implement them.

Step #7: Ask members to return to their subgroups briefly to complete any action plans that might be needed to make sure that improvements are implemented.

Priority Setting

What is it? A process for involving the members of a team or department in identifying priorities in a budget or programming cutback situation.

When should you use it? When there is a desire to involve the members of the group rather than having management determine the priorities. To benefit from the input and ideas of all staff.

What is its purpose? Helps members clarify their priorities and take responsibility for managing in a constrained environment.

What is the outcome? A set of priorities created by group members, which they're prepared to accept and to which they have a high level of commitment.

How Does Priority Setting Work?

Step #1: Identify the parameters of the priority-setting exercise. Is it to reduce budgets by 20 percent? Is it to reduce the number of products or services offered from dozens to three or four? Is it to simplify an operation? Also clarify the timelines and other realities.

If there are implications for job loss or job reassignment, these issues must be discussed openly at the start of the exercise.

Step #2: Identify all of the items that will be the focus of the priority-setting exercise. These could range from products and services to publications and office locations.

Step #3: Work together to create a list of criteria for assessing the relative importance of these items. These priority-setting criteria should be created by the group to fit the specific situation. Five to seven criteria usually will suffice.

Examples include:

- Meets customer needs/ expectations
- Supports the strategic direction
- Has top level support
- Aligns with political priorities
- Creates economic benefits
- Creates social benefits
- Creates environmental benefits
- Creates high profile
- Represents a major innovation
- Is doable/feasible
- Positive cost/benefit ratio
- Has positive impact on staff
- Contributes to program balance

Once the criteria have been identified, construct a grid with the items to be prioritized down the left-hand column and the criteria across the top. Rate each item using a scale to reflect the extent to which it meets the criteria.

The following example uses a *numerical scale* where 1 = low priority, 2 = medium priority, and 3 = high priority.

Example: If the zoo cuts its programs, what aspects should remain?

	Meets Needs of Public	Supports Strategic Direction	Creates Economic Benefits	Positive Cost/Benefit Ratio	Total Rating
Children's petting zoo	3	3	3	2.5	11.5
Guided tours	2	1	2	1	6
Guest speakers	1.75	2.5	1	1	6.25
Zoo magazine for kids	2.5	3	2	1	8.5

Step #5: Before individuals rate each item, openly discuss each item in detail. Since the final decision is made through individual ranking, this total group discussion is essential. It's especially important if jobs are at stake. In some priority-setting exercises it may be advantageous to "weight" the criteria. For details on weighting criteria, see page 163, in this chapter.

Step #6: Members then rank the items according to their understanding of how well each item meets the criteria.

Step #7: The scores are added, then divided by the number of raters, and results discussed. Discussion questions include "Did the right priorities emerge? What are the scores telling us?"

Step #8: The results of a priority-setting exercise can then be referred to a sub-committee of the larger group. It's this group's responsibility to translate the priorities into actual budget numbers and create an implementation plan. The final plan should be fed back to the whole group for ratification if the process is to remain participative.

Needs and Offers Negotiation

What is it? A constructive dialogue between two parties to identify action steps each can take to improve the relationship.

When should you use it? To encourage dialogue between parties either to resolve a conflict or to improve relations proactively before problems set in.

What is its purpose? Resolves issues in a relatively low risk manner because issues are framed as positive suggestions for improvement by both parties.

What is the outcome? A positive and constructive dialogue that lets people express past and present concerns about the relationship in totally constructive terms. Since both parties make offers, the exchange feels mutual and supportive.

How Does Needs and Offers Negotiation Work?

Step #1: Clarify who will be the focus of the exercise. This can be two separate parties, a team and its leader, two subgroups of the same team, a team and management, or two individuals.

Step #2: Set a positive climate for the exercise by talking about the value of giving and receiving feedback. Make sure that the appropriate norms are in place to encourage members to speak freely and honestly.

Step #3: Explain the process to all parties. Instruct parties that they will be separated for a period of about 20 minutes. During that time each party will think about:

        1. What I/we need from you in order to be effective

        2. What I/we offer in return to meet your needs.

The results of the deliberations are written on a flip chart.

The following example is from an exchange between a team and its leader.

Needs	Offers
What I/we need from you in order to be effective	***What I/we offer in return to meet your needs***
• More advance notice about program changes	• Full and active participation at staff meetings
• More consultation about changes that affect staff	• Getting work done on time
• Clarity regarding how much authority we have to implement	• More advance communication if things are going wrong

Step #4: When each party has written its wants and offers lists, bring parties back together to share their thoughts.

Step #5: Ask each party to withhold any comments or reactions while the other person or group presents its wants and offers. When finished, discuss their reactions. Help groups work out the action steps.

Step #6: To conclude, ask all parties to make summary statements about what their commitments and action steps will be. Put in place a process for follow-up actions.

Systematic Problem Solving

What is it? A step-by-step approach for resolving a problem or issue.

When should you use it? When members need to work together to resolve a problem.

What is its purpose? Provides a structured and disciplined means for groups to explore and resolve an issue together. An in-depth analysis ensures that groups understand their problem before jumping to solutions. This is probably the most fundamental and important facilitator tool you can employ!

What is the outcome? Systematic problem solving results in doable action steps that members of the group take responsibility for implementing. Because the process is systematic, it stops the group from randomly suggesting ideas that never get implemented. Problem solving is at the heart of collaborative conflict resolution. It's also a key activity in any organization that is dedicated to improving customer service and continuous improvement.

How Does Systematic Problem Solving Work?

Step #1: Name the problem. Identify a problem that needs to be solved. Analyze it briefly to ensure that there's a common understanding of the issue. Then support the group in writing a one- or two-sentence description of the problem. This is called the problem statement.

Step #2: Identify the goal of the problem-solving exercise. Ask the group one of the following questions: *"If this problem were totally solved, how would you describe the ideal situation"* or *"How will things look if we solve this problem?"* Summarize this in a one- to two-sentence goal statement.

Step #3: Analyze the problem. If the problem is fairly technical, do an analysis using a *Fishbone Diagram* (see page 161) . Otherwise, ask a series of probing questions to help members think analytically about the problem. Categorize the observations as either "causes" or "effects." The goal is to get to the true root causes of the problem.

Some useful questions during analysis could include:

- Describe this problem to me in detail, step by step.
- What is it? How does it manifest itself?
- What are the noticeable signs of it?
- What makes this happen?
- How are people affected?
- What other problems does it cause?
- What are the most damaging aspects?
- What stops us from solving it?
- Who gets in the way of solving it?
- What are the root causes of each symptom?

Step #4: Identify potential solutions. Use *Brainstorming* (page 155) or *Anonymous Brainstorming* (page 156) to generate potential solutions. When the ideas stop flowing, ask probing questions to encourage members to dig deeper. Some useful probing questions include:

- What if money were no object?
- What if you owned this company?
- What would the customer suggest?
- What if we did the opposite of the ideas suggested so far?
- What is the most innovative thing we could do?

Step #5: Evaluate solutions. Use either a *Criteria-Based Decision Grid* (page 162) or the *Impact//Effort Grid* (page 163) to sift through the brainstormed ideas to determine which are most applicable to the situation.

Step #6: Create an action plan. Spell out the specific steps needed to implement the best solutions. Specify how things will be done, when and by whom.

Each action step should also have some sort of a performance indicator that answers the question, "How will we know we have been successful?" This will help focus the action step and make it easier to measure results later on.

Step #8: Troubleshoot the plan. Use the *Troubleshooting* tool (page 164) to identify all of the things that could get in the way and then make sure that there are plans in place to deal with them.

Step #9: Monitor and evaluate. Identify how the action plans will be monitored and when and how the results will be reported on. Create and use a monitoring and report-back format.

You will notice that systematic problem solving incorporates many of the basic facilitation process tools.

Systematic Problem Solving Worksheet #1

Step 1.   Name the problem

Identify the problem that needs to be solved. Analyze it in just enough detail to create a common understanding. Use the space below to explore the general nature of the problem.

Now narrow in and select the specific aspect you wish to solve. Write a one- or two-sentence problem statement to define the problem clearly.

Problem statement:

_____

_____

_____

_____

Systematic Problem Solving Worksheet #2

Step 2. Identify the goal of the problem-solving exercise

Describe the desired outcome.

What would things look like if the problem disappeared? How would things look if this problem were resolved? Use the space below to record the ideas generated.

Now narrow in and write a one- or two-sentence goal statement.

Goal statement:

_____

_____

_____

_____

Systematic Problem Solving Worksheet #3

Step 3. Analyze the problem

Dissect the problem thoroughly. Avoid coming up with solutions. Instead, concentrate on making sure that everyone is clear about the specific nature of the situation. Don't focus on symptoms, but delve behind each effect to determine the root causes.

Use *Cause and Effect Charting* or a *Fishbone Diagram* (page 161) if the problem is a complex technical issue that has many contributing factors.

If you decide to use a simple questioning approach, ask:

- *How would we describe this problem to an outsider?*
- *What is taking place? What are the signs and symptoms?*
- *How are people affected? What makes this happen?*
- *What are the root causes of each symptom?*
- *What other problems does it cause?*
- *What are the most damaging aspects?*
- *What and who stops us from solving it?*
- *How do <u>we</u> contribute to the problem?*

Systematic Problem Solving Worksheet #4

Step 4. Identify potential solutions

Use *Brainstorming* (page 155) or *Anonymous Brainstorming* (page 156) to generate a list of potential solutions to the problem.

When brainstorming, remember the rules:
- let the ideas flow, be creative, don't judge
- all ideas are accepted, even if they're way-out
- build on the good ideas of others

Probing questions to ask once the group has run out of ideas:
- *what if money were no object?*
- *what if I owned this company?*
- *what would the customer suggest?*
- *what's the opposite of something already suggested?*
- *what is the most innovative thing we could do?*

Record brainstorming ideas here:

Systematic Problem Solving Worksheet #5

Step 5. Evaluate the solutions

Use the *Impact/Effort* Grid to sift through the brainstormed ideas to determine which are best for the situation.

	Effort	
	Difficult to Do	**Easy to Do**
Major Improvement	3.	1.
Minor Improvement	4.	2.

(Impact is labeled vertically along the left side of the grid.)

List all of the type 1 & 2 activities together for quick action	List all of the type 3 activities here for development into action plans

Systematic Problem Solving Worksheet #6

Step 6. Plan for action

Create detailed action plans for items that need to be implemented. Make sure action plans adhere to a logical sequence of steps. Provide details about what will be done, how and by whom. Always put in target dates for completion. Identify the performance indicator that answers the question, *"How will we know we did a good job?"*

What will be done & how?	By whom?	When?	Performance Indicator

Systematic Problem Solving Worksheet #7

Step 7. Troubleshoot the action plan

Identify all of the things that could get in the way of success in implementing the plan. Create anticipatory strategies to deal with each of the serious blockages.

Use the following questions to help identify trouble spots:

- *what are the most difficult, complex or sensitive aspects of our plan?*
- *what sudden shifts could take place to change priorities or otherwise change the environment?*
- *what organizational blocks and barriers could we run into?*
- *what technical or materials-related problems could stop or delay us?*
- *should we be aware of any human resources issues? Which ones?*
- *in which ways might members of this team not fulfill their commitments?*

What could go wrong, block us or change suddenly?	What actions do we need to take to overcome each block? (what, how, who, when, measure)

Systematic Problem Solving Worksheet #8

Step 8. Monitor and evaluate

To ensure that action plans are actually implemented, identify:

How will progress be reported?   Written _____ Verbal _____

When and how often will reports be made? _____

Who needs to be advised? _____

How will results be monitored? _____

Will there be a final report? _____

Who will take responsibility for the above actions? _____

_____

_____

Reporting on Results

What activities have been implemented?	What results have been achieved?
Remaining items	**Expected dates for completion**

Chapter 9
Process Designs

Just as an architect wouldn't dream of showing up at a construction site without a well-thought-out design, so facilitators need to create their own blueprints for each session.

In fact, one of the most important skills a facilitator needs is the ability to create meeting designs that address specific needs. Having the right process design is just as important to the success of any meeting as being able to manage the interpersonal dynamics.

On the following pages you'll find some sample process designs. These illustrate the flow of specific types of meetings and show how individual tools and techniques might be used together. Since these times and sequences are *totally speculative*, it's unlikely that any of these samples will fit real-life situations well enough to be applied straight from the book. In fact, no design should ever be borrowed from somewhere else. Part of the challenge with every group you facilitate is the creation of a custom-made design that meets the needs of that situation.

Most designs are created through a rigorous process, which usually includes:

Facilitators are expected to create unique designs that reflect the needs of any situation.

- background research — for example, reading reports and making site visits to fully understand the group's situation and history
- interviewing and/or surveying members to determine their specific goals and needs
- creating a preliminary design
- ratification of the design by a few or all members
- writing an agenda with detailed process notes
- preparation of all worksheets, handouts and overheads
- designing an appropriate evaluation form

Whether you're a full-time (professional) facilitator or not, it's important to remember that professional facilitators budget and charge as much time for research and design as they do for actually facilitating a session. This is a reminder that you shouldn't rely on sketchy session outlines, especially if you're a beginner!

Introduction to the Sample Designs

The sample agendas on the following pages are only meant to illustrate how various tools and techniques can be combined.

Each design is accompanied by a set of specifications and assumptions that explain the context for the activities chosen. All agenda items are accompanied by facilitator notes that describe the tools and techniques used. Handout materials, overheads and other props are not included in this section, although you can find many elsewhere in this book. At the conclusion of this chapter are Session Planning Worksheets to assist you with planning your next session.

Sample Process Designs	Page
1. Creating a mission statement and objectives	182
2. Work planning, roles and responsibilities	184
3. Priority setting/cutback planning	185
4. Inter-group negotiation	187
5. Finding and solving problems	189
6. Core program development	190
7. Survey feedback/IssueCensus	193
8. New leader integration	194
9. Transition planning	196
10. Process Improvement	198

Sample Design #1 — Creating a Mission Statement and Objectives

Specifications: This is a new team coming together for the first time to create a clear, common goal and specific measurable objectives. The eight members are passing acquaintances. Three hours have been set aside for this discussion.

Agenda	Process Design Notes
Welcome and agenda overview (5 minutes)	• Review the purpose of this meeting and how the three hours will be spent
Introductions (25 minutes)	• Each person chooses a partner to interview; ask name, job, skills, family info, hobbies or interest, hopes and fears about being on this team • Partners present each other to the group • Record hopes and fears
Mission statement (60 minutes)	• Present the original rationale behind the team's formation and any other available parameters • Ask members to work <u>alone</u> to answer key questions:

Agenda	Process Design Notes
	What products and services are we responsible for? *What is our unique contribution that will help the organization achieve its goals?* *What must be noteworthy about our products and services?* *In summary, what is our mission?* • After members have written their responses, have each person sit with a partner and share his/her thoughts. • After two minutes per person, have everyone find a new partner with whom to share ideas. • After two rounds, share ideas with the whole group. Synthesize ideas together. • Create a one- or two-sentence mission statement. • Post the statement on the wall.
Team Norms (10 minutes)	• Ask members: *What sorts of behaviors will make it a pleasure to be on the team? What rules should the team impose on itself to make sure that we build a positive team climate conducive to effective teamwork?* • Facilitate to pull together ideas from everyone. • Record ideas on flip chart and post on wall.
Team Objectives (80 minutes)	• Divide members into pairs, ask them to identify, without going into great detail, what the team needs to do to achieve the team's mission. • Have members share their lists with the whole group to ensure there is agreement about activities. • Provide input about how to create detailed objectives. • Ask members to work alone to write an objective for each of the identified activities. • Review and fine-tune the objectives; make sure they have been recorded for distribution.

Exit Survey	• Give members a short survey to complete before they leave. Questions can include:
	 On a scale of 1 to 5, rate:
	     How well informed do you now feel about the team?
	     How comfortable are you with the mission?
	     How appropriate and realistic are the objectives?

Adjourn	• Clarify the time, place and agenda of the next meeting.

Sample Design #2 – Work Planning, Roles and Responsibilities

<u>Specifications:</u> This is a new team that has met once to create a mission statement and objectives, but has not started to work together in closely linked roles. Three hours have been set aside for this discussion. There are eight members.

Agenda	Process Design Notes
Welcome and agenda overview (5 minutes)	• Review the purpose of this meeting and how the three hours will be spent
Review exit survey from last meeting (20 minutes)	• Post the tabulated exit survey results. • Divide the large group in half and let the sub-groups talk for five minutes on each of the questions. *What are the issues raised by the results?* and *What can we do to remedy each of the issues?* • Reassemble as a large group and share ideas for improving the team; plan for action; record ideas
Work planning (90 minutes)	• Make sure everyone has a copy of the team's objectives. Clear up any questions. Ensure members have information about items, such as budgets, at their fingertips when planning. • Ask members to identify the characteristics of a good work plan. (For example, well balanced, allows people to try new skills, etc.) • For each objective, ask people to identify what needs to be done, how and when. Allow time for individual work. • Ask individuals to write each objective and related work activities on flip chart sheets. One objective per sheet. Post sheets around the room. • Hold a discussion of each item so that members can comment, share ideas, make changes.
Roles and responsibilities (60 minutes)	• For each objective and related activities, ask members to identify the time, skills and other requirements of each activity. • Rank activities as high, medium or low, based on the degree of complexity, difficulty and time required for each. • Begin matching people with activities. Start by allowing each person to select his or her top item. Keep assigning tasks until all items are accounted for. Use the criteria to ensure that no one has all the difficult tasks, while someone else has all the simple and low time demand tasks. • Check the work plan against the criteria set at the start; ratify it and then post.
Adjourn	• Clarify the time, place and agenda of the next meeting.

Sample Design #3 – Priority Setting/Cutback Planning

<u>**Specifications:**</u> This meeting is being held in response to a management directive to cut 20 percent from the budget. Some programs have to go to make the needed cuts. The members have worked together for years in the same department. There are 18 members, plus a manager. A three-hour discussion is planned.

Agenda Process	Process Design Notes
Welcome by director (10 minutes)	• Information sharing about the purpose of the session. Encourages staff to accept the current challenge. Offers guidelines for the cutback exercise. Sets a positive tone. Q & A.
Agenda overview (5 minutes)	• Facilitator reviews the activities of the session.
Hopes, fears and norms (20 minutes)	• Facilitator asks members to choose a partner (director leaves) Partners interview each other: <u>Hopes:</u> *What's the best outcome we could hope for?* <u>Fears:</u> *What's the worst thing that could happen?* <u>Norms:</u> *What rules or guidelines do we need to impose on ourselves to make this exercise work?* • Have members share ideas and record outcome. Make sure there is a consensus on the norms. Post on a wall
Activity review (45 minutes)	• On a large, empty wall, hang several sheets of flip chart paper and draw a decision matrix chart. • Ask members to list each activity, program or service currently being offered. • Share information about each activity so that everyone understands its purpose, customers, costs, benefits, difficulty, time demands, and any other vital factors. It's a good idea to have people prepare these activity profiles ahead of time to save time at the session. • Write the activities that will be subjected to cutbacks into the left column of the decision grid.
Establish criteria (20 minutes)	• Divide the members into subgroups of three or four members. Have the subgroups identify the criteria that ought to be used to rate the activities. Refer to the process tool section of this book for examples of criteria. • Facilitate a discussion to agree on the set of criteria to be used. Use multi-voting to sort the top five criteria if too many are initially proposed.

Sample Design #3 - cont'd

Agenda	Process Design Notes
Rate the activities (20 minutes)	• Write the final criteria along the top of the decision grid. Clarify if any of the criteria should be given a greater significance than any others. Apply weights of 1x, 2x or 3x to each criteria. • Explain the voting process. Let people work out their ratings on their own in their seats. When they're done, invite people to come up to the wall and record their ratings for each program.
Discuss the ratings (30 minutes)	• Once everyone has rated the activities, add all of the scores to arrive at totals for each activity • Ask members: *What do the ratings tell us are our priority activities, programs and services? Do we agree? Are there things we should consider eliminating or at least trimming back? Do we agree?*
Propose action steps (30 minutes)	• Subdivide the members into twos and threes. Assign them each one or more of the lower-rated activities. Ask people to discuss what sorts of alterations can and should be made to that program or service to help achieve the 20 percent reduction. • Reassemble large group and share cutback ideas and get further input from the rest of the group. • Help the group make decisions and come to closure.
Adjourn	• Ensure that there are clear next steps in place. Help members identify the time, place and purpose of their next meeting.

Special Note: *In many priority-setting sessions, the participative portion of the activity ends here. Management or a small subgroup takes the information from the ranking exercise and makes the final cutback decisions. This is often a wise course of action, as it may be unfair to ask people to suggest elimination of their own jobs or roles.*

Sample Design # 4 — Inter-Group Negotiation

Specifications: This is a session with two teams who recently became embroiled in a dispute. They may be fighting over equipment, staff, customers or budgets. The team leaders have tried to settle this, but the members continue to battle on. There are eight people on each team for a total of sixteen members, including the two team leaders. There are four hours for this intervention.

Agenda	Process Design Notes
Welcome, agenda overview (15 minutes)	• Information is shared about the purpose of the session and how it came about. Team leaders speak to the members about the need to cooperate and approach this with a collaborative mind-set. The details of each step in the negotiation are discussed.
Introductions (30 minutes)	• Create pairs, with one person from each team; ask people to interview each other to get information such as name, job or role, special interests or hobbies, and anything else that's relevant. • Members present their partners to the whole group.
Team presentations (20 minutes)	• Give teams 10 minutes each to do a brief presentation about the team: what they do, their customers, their successes, etc.

Hopes, fears, norms (30 minutes)	• Everyone finds a new partner on the other team to discuss:
	    Hopes: What's the best outcome we could hope for today?
	    Fears: What's the worst thing that could happen today?
	    Norms: How should we conduct ourselves today to ensure that relations don't worsen?
	• Have members share ideas and record the outcomes. Ask challenging questions and make suggestions to ensure that a complete set of norms is developed.

Perception sharing (40 minutes)	• Briefly explain the rules and language of giving feedback to ensure that everyone is clear how feedback is different from criticism. • Give teams twenty minutes or so to create a point-form description of the current situation. They can describe exactly what happened, when and what the impacts of those actions were. • Separate the group, preferably in different rooms, while they talk to construct their sides of the story. Have each team choose a spokesperson to present its side. • Reunite the two teams and explain that while one group talks the other team members can't interrupt or use negative body language. They must listen to what the other team is saying even if they disagree totally. They can, however, ask clarifying questions.

Sample Design #4 (cont'd)

Agenda	Process Design Notes
Perception sharing, cont'd (40 minutes)	• Ask one side to tell the other their perception of what is causing tensions. When the team is finished, the spokesperson from the other team offers a summary of what's been said, paraphrasing only his or her understanding, not agreeing or disagreeing. This step is purely a listening/understanding exercise. • Repeat the process with the second team.

Wants and offers (30 minutes)	• Once each team indicates that the other team has accurately understood what each has presented, the teams are separated again.
	• Each team chooses a facilitator to discuss the following two items on which they will report back to the rest of the group:
	    What do we need from the other team to resolve this situation?
	    What are we prepared to do to resolve the situation?
	• The teams return to the large room and take turns presenting their wants and offers to each other. Again the spokesperson for the listening team paraphrases what was said to make sure there are no misunderstandings.

Action planning (40 minutes)	• Once everyone has heard the wants and offers of the other team, the facilitator leads a discussion to negotiate final actions and help members create doable action plans that will help resolve the tensions. • Finalize the action plans and make sure there is a time and date set to meet with team spokespersons to follow up.
Adjourn	Ensure that there are clear next steps in place. Help members identify the time, place and purpose of their next meeting.

Sample Design #5 — Finding and Solving Problems

Specifications: This meeting is being held to identify and solve recurring problems being experienced by a department. The 20 members have been working together for some time. There are three hours for this activity.

Agenda	Process Design Notes
Welcome and agenda overview (5 minutes)	• Review the purpose of the meeting and how the three hours will be spent. • Review the group's norms. • Clarify any parameters or limits, like spending ceilings, that may impact the problem-solving activity. Also clarify how empowered members are to solve this problem.
Clarify the focus (5 minutes)	• Have someone briefly describe the program, service or activity that is being explored. Make sure everyone is clear on what is being discussed.

Force-field analysis
(20 minutes)
	• Have members draw on their experience and any data gathered before the session to respond to the force-field questions:
	    What are we doing really well, and what should we keep doing the same way?
	    What aren't we doing well, and what needs to improve?

Multi-voting (20 minutes)	• Once the problems are listed and understood by all members, create criteria for identifying which blocks should be removed first. The voting criteria could be the biggest blocks, or the easiest to remove. • Hand out peel-off dots or distribute points; let members vote. • Tally the votes to reveal the ranking of the blocks.
Problem solving (90 minutes)	• Take the top 3 or 4 blocks and subdivide the large group into subgroups to tackle one problem each. • Explain the steps in the Systematic Problem-Solving Model. Give out the worksheets. Have each subgroup appoint a facilitator. • Circulate among the groups to make sure they don't get stuck on any parts of the model.
Plenary (40 minutes)	• Bring groups together at the end to share their recommendations and action plans. Invite others in the group to add their ideas. • Have subgroups refine their plans and submit them to the minute taker. • Help the group plan its follow-up mechanism to ensure there are report-backs on progress made.
Adjourn	Ensure that there are clear next steps in place. Help members identify the time, place and purpose of their next meeting.

Sample Design # 6 — Core Program Development

Specifications: This is a session for a long-established department or division within an organization that has lost its focus. The members now wish to review what they're doing and get back on track to achieve their main business. All of the members know each other. There are 24 people, and the session is planned to last from 8:30 a.m. to 4:30 p.m.

Agenda	Process Design Notes
Welcome and agenda overview (5 minutes)	• Review the purpose of the meeting and how the day will be managed.
Context setting (25 minutes)	• Senior manager puts the core program challenge into clear context, clarifies the empowerment of the group to make recommendations and take action, and his or her hope and fears. • Question and answer session to get clarity on any issues members may have.

Hopes, fears and norms (20 minutes)	• Facilitator asks everyone to choose a partner. Partners interview each other:
	    Hopes: What would be the best outcome today?
	    Fears: What's the worst thing that could happen?
	    Norms: What rules or guidelines should we impose on ourselves to overcome the potential pitfalls of a core business discussion?
	• Partners report back information discussed.
	• Flip chart norms for setting group parameters.

Environmental scan (30 minutes)	• In the same room, divide members into subgroups of six people. Ask each group to choose a facilitator. Have them discuss: *What is happening around us? (In the marketplace/community/government, etc.) What trends will impact on us?* • Hold a brief plenary to share ideas between the subgroups. • Synthesize all ideas together on a flip chart • Post summary on the wall.

Customer profile (30 minutes)	• The same subgroups choose a new facilitator and discuss:
	    Who are our customers today? (describe)
	    Who will our customers be tomorrow? Who are those customers — what do they want/need?
	• Hold a brief plenary to share ideas.
	• Post the customer profile.

Sample Design # 6 (cont'd)

Agenda	Process Design Notes

Current focus
(30 minutes)
	• Ask subgroups to create a profile in response to the question:
	   What business are we currently in?
	   What are our current products and services?
	• When the products and services list is complete, pull together a complete list and write down the left-hand column of a *Criteria-Based Decision Grid*.
	• Post the grid, but don't develop it further at this time.

Strengths analysis (30 minutes)	• Have members return to subgroups and choose the next facilitator to discuss: *What are our current strengths and capabilities? What are we especially skilled at?* • Hold a brief plenary to share ideas between groups. Post strengths analysis.
Visioning (60 minutes)	• Reassemble entire group and ask each person to find a blank piece of paper. Allow up to ten minutes for individuals to answer the following questions without talking to another member. Imagine that today is exactly three years from now and we are hugely successful: *What business are we in? Describe our products and services. Who are our customers? What distinguishes us from the competition? What specific results have we achieved?* • Once individuals indicate that they have answered the questions, have everyone find a partner and proceed as per the instructions for *Visioning*. • Facilitate a plenary discussion to synthesize ideas. Ensure there is clarity about the desired future of the organization. • Help members write a statement that describes what their core business needs to be. • Post the statement and key points on the wall.
Mid-point check	• Post a mid-point check survey on the wall and ask members to respond to the questions as they leave for lunch or a break. These can be about progress being made, the process, the pace, etc. • When the meeting resumes, review the ratings and make improvements.
Ranking products and services (45 minutes)	• Return to the decision grid. Down the left side add any future activities, products or services that were agreed to in the visioning exercise.

Sample Design #6 (cont'd)

Agenda	Process Design Notes

Ranking products and services, cont'd (45 minutes)	• Facilitate a discussion to establish criteria to rank the items. Potential criteria can include:
	    • Supports the core business
	    • High profitability
	    • Builds on current strengths
	    • Meets a growing customer need, etc.
	• Write the criteria along the top of the decision grid, then other items. Assign weights of 1x, 2x, and 3x.
	• Have each person do his or her own ranking. Then ask members to write their rankings on the chart.

Ranking analysis (80 minutes)	• When all rankings are tabulated, ask subgroups to hold discussions to analyze the rankings:
	    What do the rankings tell us we should be focusing on in support of our core business?
	    What do we need to start doing?
	    What do we need to keep on doing?
	    What do we need to stop doing?
	• Facilitate a plenary to synthesize ideas and reach agreement on priorities for action.
	• Categorize activities/programs/services under three headings:
	New activities that need to be developed;
	Existing activities to be trimmed;
	Existing activities to be eliminated.

Strategy development (90 minutes)	• Post the activities under the three headings and let members sort themselves according to their skills, interests and knowledge. • Have subgroups take responsibility for developing action plans that develop new opportunities, reduce activity or divest programs. The process for strategy development can center around the following questions: *What's involved in starting/trimming/stopping this activity? List steps. Who's likely going to be affected? What are the implications? What's the likely cost/benefit? What are the next steps: what should be done, how, by whom, when, and with what result?* • Hold a plenary to share ideas and have all action plans ratified by the whole group. • Help the group members identify how and when they will monitor and report on progress.
Evaluation (20 minutes)	• Evaluate member satisfaction by asking each person to comment on his or her feelings about the day. Compare these with hopes and fears set at the start.
Adjourn	• Ensure that there are clear next steps in place. Help members identify the time, place and purpose of their next meeting.

Sample Design #7 — Survey Feedback/Issue Census

Specifications: A division or department within an organization wishes to identify its issues using a survey. This can be an employee satisfaction survey, a customer satisfaction survey or a survey of the performance of a product or process. There are 36 people, who have been working together for some time, at this three-hour survey feedback meeting. The survey being discussed was conducted in the weeks preceding this meeting; results were tabulated and a copy of the final tally sheets was given, without interpretation, to all members.

Agenda Process	Process Design Notes
Welcome and agenda overview (5 minutes)	• Review of the purpose of the session and explanation of the survey feedback method.
Review survey results (25 minutes)	• Lead the whole group through a review of each question. Discuss: *Is this a high or low rating? Is everyone clear about what this question meant?* • Without interpreting the results, sort the responses into three categories: Items scored as good or high; Items scored as poor or low; Borderline items.

Interpreting the results (60 minutes)	• Divide the members into subgroups of six members.
	 • Ask each subgroup to appoint a facilitator. Give each group only one issue to work on.
	 • Groups are to work through the following questions and steps in connection with their survey item:
	   • *Why did these items get such low ratings?* (analyze the situation)
	   • *What are some actions that could improve these ratings?* (brainstorm solutions)
	   • *Which of our solutions do we think are most promising?* (impact/effort grid or decision grid)

Plenary (60 minutes)	• Have members share their assessments, in order to benefit from each other's comments, and ratify the solutions being proposed.
Action planning (30 minutes)	• Have members return to their original subgroups to develop action plans for ideas ratified by the larger group.
Plenary (30 minutes)	• Ask subgroups to inform the rest of the members of their specific action plans for implementing the discussed improvements. • Make sure members have a plan for monitoring, reporting and follow-up. • Evaluate the effectiveness of the session.
Adjourn	

Sample Design # 8 – New Leader Integration

<u>Specifications:</u> An established team or department, with a good track record, is about to receive a new leader. The organization is concerned that the new leader be integrated quickly. It's also hoped that the transition be smooth. The new leader integration session is conducted in stages over a period of three hours. Any number of staff can attend. The first stage takes place the week before the leader joins the group.

Agenda Process	Process Design Notes
Stage 1 Welcome and agenda overview (10 minutes)	• At a preliminary planning session not attended by the leader, review the purpose of the new leader integration session and explain the process.

Profile preparation
(90 minutes)
	• Ask members to prepare a profile of the group. This profile will be given to the new leader in advance of a joint session. It should include:
	    • *Who are we? (Our purpose, products/services, staff/skills)*
	    • *What are we most proud of?*
	    • *What are we doing very well at this time? Why are we doing so well in this area?*
	    • *What aren't we doing that well? Why not?*
	    • *What are we doing to improve?*
	    • *What's ahead for us in six months, one year, three years?*
	    • *Under what leadership style do we work best? Why?*
	    • *How empowered have we been/should we be? For which activities?*
	    • *What do we need from our new leader?*
	    • *What are we offering our new leader?*
	• The notes from this discussion should be recorded and typed for distribution.

Stage 2 Leader preparation	• The facilitator meets with the new leader and brings him/her the group profile. The leader is asked to read the profile, prepare one about him/herself along the same lines, and be ready to discuss his/her leadership style and philosophy of empowerment. • The leader is asked to be ready to discuss what he/she needs from the group and what he/she's prepared to offer.
Stage 3 Welcome and agenda overview (10 minutes)	• At the meeting of the members and the new leader, review the steps of the process.
Member presentation (60 minutes)	• Members are given the opportunity of speaking first to share their profile, needs and offers.

Sample Design # 8 (cont'd)

Agenda Process	Process Design Notes
Member presentation, cont'd (60 minutes)	• The leader is asked to listen and ask clarifying questions only.
Leader presentation (30 minutes)	• The leader is given the opportunity of presenting his/her profile, including leadership style, wants and offers, etc. Members are asked to listen and ask questions.
Discussions and negotiations (30 minutes)	• Once both parties have heard each other, the facilitator manages a discussion of any of the points where there appear to be differences or a need for further exploration. • If any item needs an action plan, the facilitator can help the group identify its next steps.
Adjourn	• Have a coffee break planned to encourage social mixing.

Sample Design # 9 — Transition Planning

Specifications: A division or a department within an organization is about to undergo major change. Some staff will trade jobs. Others will trade territories. Some people will gain new titles. Others will need to acquire new skills. This planning exercise is being conducted to ensure that nothing slips between the cracks and that customer service levels remain high during the actual changeover period. Twenty-four people are involved. A full day has been set aside for the transition discussion.

Agenda Process	Process Design Notes
Welcome and agenda overview (5 minutes)	• Review the purpose of the meeting and how the session will be conducted.

Buy-in to the process (30 minutes)	• Have everyone find a partner to interview. Pose the following questions for partners to ask each other:
	    • *Why is it important that we have a transition plan?*
	    • *Why should we be the ones to create it?*
	    • *What would be the best possible outcome?*
	    • *What would be the worst outcome?*
	    • *What norms or rules should we impose on ourselves today to make sure that we create a fair plan everyone can live with?*
	• Facilitate a discussion to gather up major thoughts and post these.

Information sharing (45 minutes)	• Presentations by those driving the change, detailing what needs to happen and when. • Question and answer session.

Identifying challenges (45 minutes)	• Divide the members by existing work groups if applicable, or create random subgroups of three to four members.
	• Ask them to use *force-field analysis* to identify:
	    • *What aspects of the change are going to be relatively simple/easy?*
	    • *What aspects of the change are going to be complicated/challenging?*
	• Hold a plenary to create a common force field.
	• Use multi-voting to rank the challenges from most to least complicated/challenging.

Strategy development (120 minutes)	• Help the whole group identify the characteristics of an effective transition. This can include things such as, "doesn't disrupt customer service" or "allows people to get on-the-job coaching," etc. • Post these criteria. • Take the top four changes that were ranked to be most challenging or complicated and post these at four places around the room. • Ask members to go to the "change challenge" that involves them so that people who will be responsible for implementing each plan are in each group.

Sample Design #9 (cont'd)

Agenda Process	Process Design Notes
Strategy development, cont'd (120 minutes)	• Ask each subgroup to identify a facilitator and hold a strategy development discussion. • The following discussions make up this process: 1. Describe the old state —*What activities/products/services are involved? What skills, roles and responsibilities are associated with each activity?* 2. Describe the new state — *What activities/products/services define the future state? For each activity: what are the skills, roles and responsibilities? What are the implementation dates? What is negotiable versus non-negotiable? What can go wrong?* 3. Transition planning — *Given the time frames, is there a logical sequence of steps for implementing the change in stages? How many hand-offs are there? How can these be handled to ensure continuity? Given the new roles, who needs training/on-the-job coaching? What signals can be put in place to help us monitor the transition to ensure things don't go too far off track?*
Plenary (60 minutes)	• Have subgroups share their proposed transition plans. Encourage others to offer comments to fill in any gaps in the plans. Make sure the subgroup plans are linked together to form a coherent whole. Check carefully for clarity and true consensus. Ensure that sensitive change issues are discussed and brought to proper closure.
Action planning (60 minutes)	• Have subgroups fill out action planning sheets that identify what will be done, how, by whom and when. • Bring groups together one last time to hear each other's action plans. Ensure that notes are available for distribution soon after the meeting.
Communications planning (30 minutes)	• Ask members to identify who needs to be given information about the transition plan. • Record the communications strategy, specifying who needs to know what and when. • Ensure that clear responsibility is taken for communicating the details of the transition.
Monitoring (15 minutes)	• Help the group identify how it will monitor the plan and report on progress. • Set a date for the next meeting. • Go around the room and ask members how they felt about the day.
Adjourn	

Sample Design #10 — Process Improvement

<u>*Specifications:*</u> A work group has received information that one of its key product/services/activities is problematic. The week before the session, a subgroup meets for three hours to prepare a process map showing each step of the current process. When the map is complete, key internal stakeholders and selected external customers are interviewed to gain their perspective on how the process currently functions. Eighteen people, who know each other well, will be at the session; about three hours is available to find viable improvement ideas.

Agenda Process	Process Design Notes
Welcome and agenda overview (5 minutes)	• Review the purpose of the meeting and how the session will be conducted.
Buy-in and norms (15 minutes)	• Ask members to find a partner to discuss two questions: 　• *Why is it important to improve this particular process?* 　• *What rules should we set for ourselves today to make sure we reach consensus on improvements that will really make a difference?* • Facilitate a plenary to synthesize together the ideas of the partners. • Post key ideas and norms.
Map review (45 minutes)	• Ask the members who constructed the process map to explain all of the steps they identified. • Encourage the rest of the members to ask questions and add any missing details. • Ratify that the map is acceptable to all present. • Have members who did the interviews hand out copies of the data gathered and share highlights. Encourage questioning by others.
Forcefield analysis (45 minutes)	• Facilitate the whole group in a force-field analysis exercise as they identify: 　• *What does the data tell us is working well? What is fine as it is?* 　• *What does the data tell us isn't working well? What needs improvement?* • Use multi-voting to identify the priority issues that need to be resolved by this group at this day's session.
Problem solving (60 minutes)	• Post the top three issues in different parts of the room. • Ask members to divide themselves into groups based on interest and knowledge to work on these issues. • Review the steps of the problem-solving model and ask subgroups to select one or more facilitators to manage the session. • Hold a plenary to share recommendations and ratify action plans.
Next steps (10 minutes)	• Ensure that a time and date have been set for the next meeting to follow up on the action plans. • Evaluate the session.

Session Planning Worksheet

To aid you in planning your next session, consider the following:

Purpose of the session: _____

_____

Number of members: _____ Do they need to be introduced? Y / N

1. What will you do to warm the group up to the task?

_____

_____

_____

2. Do you need to develop special targeted norms for this activity? If yes, what should the norming question be?

_____

_____

_____

3. Will buy-in be a problem? If yes, what is the buy-in question you should ask?

_____

_____

_____

4. What background information, empowerment parameters or other constraints do members need to know about?

_____

_____

_____

_____

_____

5. What are the key questions that need to be answered in order to arrive at the answers the group will be seeking?

_____

_____

_____

_____

_____

_____

Session Planning Worksheet (cont'd)

6. What activities/process tools do you expect to be using at the session?

_____
_____
_____
_____
_____
_____
_____

7. What could go wrong at the session? (Possible considerations: interpersonal conflicts, cynicism, lack of energy, overwhelming task, unable to achieve closure, lack of skills, etc.) For each possible problem, also identify strategies to overcome it.

Session Barriers	Solutions

8. What evaluation questions should you plan to ask at the start?

_____
_____
_____
_____

At the mid-point check?

_____
_____
_____

On the final evaluation form?

_____
_____
_____

9. What audiovisual aids, videos, and other props will you need?

_____
_____
_____
_____

About the Author

*I*ngrid Bens is a consultant and trainer whose primary areas of focus are conflict management, team building, facilitation, leadership and organizational change. Ingrid has a master's degree in adult education and over twenty years' experience facilitating team implementation and process improvement efforts in the public, private and non-profit sectors.

When not consulting on change projects, Ingrid divides her time between teaching in-house workshops for clients and presenting at conferences for the University of North Texas' Center for the Study of Work Teams, the Association for Quality and Participation, Linkage Incorporated and the Banff Center for Management.

For information about workshops go to: www.participative-dynamics.com

Acknowledgments

*M*any people helped me prepare this book. In particular I wish to thank those colleagues who reviewed the original manuscript and added their valuable comments: Bev Davids, Carl Aspler, Charlotte de Heinrich and Charles Bens. I also wish to thank the person who served as my original mentor, Marilyn Laiken, professor of adult education at the Ontario Institute for Studies in Education (Toronto) for her guidance and for being a clear role model of what a facilitator can and should be.

The final manuscript received tremendous help from consulting partner Michael Goldman, who provided ongoing editorial assistance, and from Mary House, who created the original cover design and easy-to-read layout of this book. Special thanks also to the editorial staff at Jossey-Bass, especially Susan Williams, Julianna Gustafson, Pamela Berkman, and Deb Nasitka.

Bibliography

Chapter 1

Argyris, C. (1970) *Intervention Theory and Method.* Addison-Wesley. Reading, Mass.

Beckhard, R. (1969) *Organization Development: Strategies and Models.* Addison-Wesley. Reading, Mass.

Bennis, W.G. (1966) *Changing Organizations.* McGraw-Hill. New York.

Block, P. (1999) *Flawless Consulting,* (2nd ed.) Jossey-Bass/Pfeiffer. San Francisco.

Block, P. (1987) *The Empowered Manager.* Jossey-Bass. San Francisco.

French, W.L., & Bell, C. H., Jr. (1978) *Organization Development.* Prentice Hall. Englewood Cliffs, N.J.

Hargrove, R. (1995) *Masterful Coaching.* Jossey-Bass/Pfeiffer. San Francisco.

Jongewood, D., & James, M. (1973) *Winning with People.* Addison-Wesley. Reading, Mass.

Kayser, T.A. (1990) *Mining Group Gold.* Serif Publishing. Sequndo, Calif.

Lewin, K., & Hanson, P. *Giving Feedback: An Interpersonal Skill.* In Bennis, W.G. and others. (1976) *The Planning of Change* (3rd ed). Holt Rinehart & Winston. New York.

Lippit, G.L. (1969) *Organization Renewal.* Appleton, Century, Crofts. New York.

McKroskey, J.C.; Larson, C.E.; & Knapp, M.L. (1971) *An Introduction to Interpersonal Communication.* Prentice Hall. Englewood Cliffs, N.J.

Nadler, D.A. (1977) *Feedback and Organization Development.* Addison-Wesley. Reading, Mass.

Schein, E. H., & Bennis, W. G. (1965) *Personal and Organization Change Through Group Methods: The Laboratory Approach.* Wiley. New York.

Schein, E. H. (1969) *Process Consultation: Its Role in Organization Development.* Addison-Wesley. Reading, Mass.

Schein, E. H. (1987) *Process Consultation: Lessons for Managers and Consultants.* Addison-Wesley. Reading, Mass.

Chapter 2

Argyris, C . (1970) *Intervention Theory and Method.* Addison-Wesley. Reading, Mass.

Beckhard, R. (1969) *Organization Development: Strategies and Models.* Addison-Wesley. Reading, Mass.

Blake, R.R., & Mouton, J.S. (1968) *Corporate Excellence Through Grid Organization Development.* Gulf. Houston, Tex.

Block, P. (1999) *Flawless Consulting.* Jossey-Bass/Pfeiffer. San Francisco.

Lewin, K., & Hanson, P. *Giving Feedback: An Interpersonal Skill.* In Bennis, W.G. and others. (1976) *The Planning of Change* (3rd ed). Holt Rinehart & Winston. New York.

Likert, R. (1967) *The Human Organization.* McGraw-Hill. New York.

Lippitt, G., & Lippitt, R. (1978) *The Consulting Process in Action.* Jossey-Bass/Pfeiffer. San Francisco.

Margulies, N., & Wallace, J. (1973) *Organizational Change: Techniques and Applications.* Scott, Foresman. Glenview, Ill.

Nadler, D.A. (1977) *Feedback and Organization Development.* Addison-Wesley. Reading, Mass.

Reddy, B. (1994) *Intervention Skills: Process Consultation for Small Groups and Teams.* Jossey-Bass/Pfeiffer. San Francisco.

Schein, E.H. (1969) *Process Consultation: Its Role in Organization Development.* Addison-Wesley. Reading, Mass.

Schein, E.H. (1987) *Process Consultation: Lessons for Managers and Consultants.* Addison-Wesley. Reading, Mass.

Chapter 3

Argyris, C. (1964) *Integrating the Individual and the Organization.* Wiley. New York.

Beckhard, R., & Harris, R.T. (1969) *Organizational Transitions: Managing Complex Change.* Addison-Wesley. Reading, Mass.

Dyer, W.G. (1987) *Team Building.* Addison-Wesley. Reading, Mass.

Likert, R. (1961) *New Patterns of Management.* McGraw-Hill. New York.

McGregor, D. (1960) *The Human Side of Enterprise.* McGraw-Hill. New York.

Pfieffer, J.W., & Jones, J.E. (1972) *A Handbook of Structured Experiences for Human Relations Training* (vols I–X).

Schutz, W.C. (1966) *The Interpersonal Underworld.* Science and Behavior Books. Palo Alto, Calif.

Schein, E.H. (1969) *Process Consultation.* Addison-Wesley. Reading, Mass.

Tuckman, B.W. (1965) Development Sequences in Small Groups. *Psychological Bulletin.*

Weisbord, M.M. (1991) *Productive Workplaces.* Jossey-Bass. San Francisco.

Chapter 4

Bennis, W.G. (1966) *Changing Organizations.* McGraw-Hill. New York.

Bennis, W.G. and others. (1976) *The Planning of Change* (3rd ed). Holt Rinehart & Winston. New York.

French, W.L., & Bell, C.H., Jr. (1978) *Organization Development.* Prentice Hall. Englewood Cliffs, N.J.

Kayser, T.A. (1990) *Mining Group Gold.* Serif Publishing. Sequndo, Calif.

Pfieffer, J.W., & Jones, J.E. (1972) *A Handbook of Structured Experiences for Human Relations Training* (vol I–X). Jossey-Bass/Pfeiffer. San Francisco.

Scannell, E. E., & Newstrom, J. (1991) *Still More Games Trainers Play.* McGraw-Hill. New York.

Schein, E. H., & Bennis, W. G. (1965) *Personal and Organization Change Through Group Methods: The Laboratory Approach.* Wiley. New York.

Schein, E.H. (1969) *Process Consultation: Its Role in Organization Development.* Addison-Wesley. Reading, Mass.

Schein, E. H. (1987) *Process Consultation: Lessons for Managers and Consultants.* Addison-Wesley. Reading, Mass.

Senge, P., and others. (1994) *Fifth Discipline Fieldbook.* Doubleday. New York.

Wood, J.T., Phillips, G., & Pederson, D.J. (1986) *Group Discussion: a Practical Guide to Participation and Leadership.* Harper and Row. New York.

Chapter 5:

Beckhard, R. (March 1967) The Confrontation Meeting. *Harvard Business Review 45.*

Beckhard, R. (1969) *Organization Development: Strategies and Models.* Addison-Wesley. Reading, Mass.

Blake, R.R., Shepard, H., & Mouton, J.S. (1965) *Managing Intergroup Conflict in Industry.* Gulf Publishing. Houston, Tex.

Fisher, R., & Ury, W. (1983) *Getting to Yes.* Penguin Books. New York.

Filley, A. C. (1975) *Interpersonal Conflict Resolution.* Scott, Foresman. Glenview, Ill.

Kilmann, R.H., & Thomas, K.W. (1978) Four Perspectives on Conflict Management: An Attributional Framework for Organizing Descriptive and Normative Theory. *Academy of Management Review.*

Kindler, H.S. (1988) *Managing Disagreement Constructively.* Crisp Publications. Los Altos, Calif.

Likert, R., & Likert, J.G. (1976) *New Ways of Managing Conflict.* McGraw-Hill. New York.

Walton, R.E. (1987) *Managing Conflict: Interpersonal Dialogue and Third Party Roles.* Addison-Wesley. Reading, Mass.

Thomas, K.W., & Kilmann, R.H. (1974) *The Thomas Kilmann Conflict Mode Instrument.* Xicom. Tuxedo, N.Y.

Chapter 6

Avery, M., Auvine, B., Streiel, B., & Weiss, L. (1981) *Building United Judgment: A Handbook for Consensus Decision Making.* The Center for Conflict Resolution. Madison, Wis.

DeBono, E. (1985) *Six Thinking Hats.* Key Porter Books. Toronto.

DeBono, E. (1993) *Serious Creativity.* HarperCollins. New York.

Fisher, A.B. (1974) *Small Group Decision Making: Communication and Group Process.* McGraw-Hill. New York.

Fisher R., & Ury, W. (1983) *Getting to Yes.* Penguin Books. New York.

Harvey, J.B. (1988) *The Abilene Paradox and Other Meditations on Management.* Heath. Lexington, Mass.

Kuhn, T.S. (1970) *The Structure of Scientific Revolutions.* University of Chicago Press. Chicago.

Schneider, W.E. (1994) *The Reengineering Alternative: A Plan for Making Your Current Culture Work.* Irwin. Burr Ridge, Ill.

Van Gundy, A.B. (1981) *Techniques of Structured Problem Solving.* Van Nostrand Reinhold. New York.

Chapter 7

Bradford, L.P. (1976) *Making Meetings Work.* Jossey-Bass/Pfeiffer. San Francisco.

Doyle, M., & Straus, D. (1976) *How to Make Meetings Work: The New Interaction Method.* Berkley Publishing Group. New York.

Dyer, W.G. (1987) *Team Building.* Addison-Wesley. Reading, Mass.

Frank, M. O. (1989) *How to Run a Meeting in Half the Time.* Simon and Schuster. New York.

Haynes, M. E. (1988) *Effective Meeting Skills: A Practical Guide for More Productive Meetings.* Crisp Publications. Los Altos, Calif.

Jones, J. E. (1980) Dealing with the Disruptive Individuals in Meetings: *The 1980 Annual Handbook for Group Facilitators.* Jossey-Bass/Pfeiffer. San Francisco.

Chapter 8

Beckhard, R. (1969) *Organization Development: Strategies and Models.* Addison-Wesley. Reading, Mass.

Delbecq, A.L., & Van de Ven, A. H. (1971) A Group Process Model for Problem Identification and Problem Planning. *Journal of Applied Behavioral Science.*

Deming, W. E. (1986) *Out of Crisis.* MIT Center for Advanced Engineering Study. Cambridge, Mass.

Fritz, R. (1990) *The Path of Least Resistance.*

Fritz, R. (1991) *Creating.* Fawcett Columbine. New York.

Green, T.B., & D.F., R. (1973) *Management in an Age of Rapid Technological and Social Change.* Southern Management Association Proceedings. Houston, Tex.

Ingle, S. (1982) *Quality Circle Masters Guide.* Prentice Hall. Englewood Cliffs, N.J.

Ishikawa, K. (1990) *Introduction to Quality Control.* 3A Corporation. Tokyo.

Massarik, F. (1990) *Advances in Organization Development.* Ablex Publishing Corporation. Orwood, N.J.

Ouchi, W. (1981) *Theory Z.* Addison-Wesley. Reading, Mass.

Pfieffer, J.W., & Jones, J.E. (1972) *A Handbook of Structured Experiences for Human Relations Training* (vol I–X). Jossey-Bass/Pfeiffer. San Francisco.

Senge, P., and others. (1994) *Fifth Discipline Fieldbook.* Doubleday. New York.

How to Use the CD-ROM

System Requirements

Windows PC
- 486 or Pentium processor-based personal computer
- Microsoft Windows 95, or Windows NT 3.51 or later
- Minimum RAM: 8 MB for Windows 95 and NT
- Available space on hard disk: 8 MB Windows 95 and NT
- 2X speed CD-ROM drive or faster
- Netscape 3.0 or higher browser or MS Internet Explorer 3.0 or higher

Macintosh
- Macintosh with a 68020 or higher processor or Power Macintosh
- Apple OS version 7.0 or later
- Minimum RAM: 12 MB for Macintosh
- Available space on hard disk: 6MB Macintosh
- 2X speed CD-ROM drive or faster
- Netscape 3.0 or higher browser or MS Internet Explorer 3.0 or higher

NOTE: This CD requires Netscape 3.0 or MS Internet Explorer 3.0 or higher. You can download these products using the links on the CD-ROM Help Page.

Getting Started

Insert the CD-ROM into your drive. The CD-ROM will usually launch automatically. If it does not, click on the CD-ROM drive on your computer to launch. You will see an opening page. You can click on this page or wait for it to fade to the Copyright Page. After you click to agree to the terms of the Copyright Page, the Home Page will appear.

Moving Around

Use the buttons at the left of each screen or the underlined text at the bottom of each screen to move among the menu pages. To view a document listed on one of the menu pages, simply click on the name of the document. To quit a document at any time, click the box at the upper right-hand corner of the screen.

Use the scrollbar at the right of the screen to scroll up and down each page.

To quit the CD-ROM, you can click the Quit button on each menu page or hit Control-Q.

To Download Documents

Open the document you wish to download. Under the File pulldown menu, choose Save As. Save the document c   your hard drive with a different name. It is important to use a different name, otherwise the document may remain a   nly file.

You can also click on your CD drive in Windows Explorer and select a document to copy it to your hard driv rename it.

In Case of Trouble

If you experience difficulty using the *Facilitating with Ease!* CD-ROM, please follow these steps:

1. Make sure your hardware and systems configurations conform to the systems requirements noted under "S, Requirements" above.
2. Review the installation procedure for your type of hardware and operating system. It is possible to reinstall tl ware if necessary.
3. You may call Jossey-Bass or Jossey-Bass/Pfeiffer Customer Service at (415) 433-1740 between the hours of 8 A.N 5 P.M. Pacific Time, and ask for Jossey-Bass CD-ROM Technical Support.
   Please have the following information available:
   - Type of computer and operating system
   - Version of Windows or Mac OS being used
   - Any error messages displayed
   - Complete description of the problem

(It is best if you are sitting at your computer when making the call.)